RITUALS

Simple & Radical Practices For

Enchantment In Times Of Crisis

YARROW MAGDALENA

www.YarrowMagdalena.com

www.YarrowDigital.com

www.Patreon.com/DaydreamingWolves

© 2020 Yarrow Magdalena

All rights reserved. No portion of this book may be reproduced in any form without permission from the publisher

I dedicate his book to Scottish landscapes. Writing *Rituals* was the very least I could do to say thank you for welcoming me with so much kindness and for holding me through the uncertainty and loneliness of a pandemic.

TABLE OF CONTENTS

Introduction 1

Part I - Elements Of Ritual 11

    Enchantment 12

    Ritual & Mental Health 15

    Cultural Appropriation 18

    Reciprocity 20

    Accessibility 24

    Grounding & Protection 25

    Altars 28

    Working With The Elements 29

    Ancestors 31

    Death Awareness 34

    Activism & Justice 38

    Rituals With Others 39

    Working With The Moon 42

    Intentions & Affirmations 43

    Folk Herbalism 45

    Journeying 47

    Meditation 50

    Divination 51

    Embodiment 53

    Writing And Other Creative Expressions 55

Part II - Ritual Practices 58

Rituals For Heartbreak, Grief And Loss 60

    Making Literal Space For Grief 61

    Letting The Sea Receive Your Sad Stuff 63

    Crying In The Rain 64

    Working With Stillness 64

    Small Rituals To Hold Ourselves 66

    Remembering Extinction 67

Rituals For New Chapters, Identities And Transitions 69

    Marrying Yourself 73

    Choosing A New Name 75

    Home Blessings & Home Goodbyes 76

    Gender Rites Of Passage 78

    Letter Writing As A Ritual 82

    Rituals For Illnesses And Disabilities 83

Rituals For Body Blessings 87

    A Mirror Ritual 91

    Becoming A Flowery Body Of Water 92

    Rituals Of Safe Touch 93

    A Spell For Protection & Visibility 95

    A Ritual To Get Unstuck 98

    Water Rituals 99

    Becoming Present 101

Meeting The Pain 103

Rituals For Creativity 105

Weaving Or Stitching For Repair 108

Writing With Tarot Cards 110

Zine Making 111

Morning Pages 113

Digital Collaging 115

Rituals For Enchantment And Resilience 117

Small Commitment Ceremonies 119

Making A Local Plant Friend 121

Inhabiting An Archetype 123

Forests As Altars, Oceans As Temples 123

Rituals For Mutual Unshaming 125

Deepening Intimacy With What We Already Have 128

Dark Moon Magic 130

Finding A Good Place For Your Inner Child 132

Part III - Creating A Regular Practice To Lean Into 135

INTRODUCTION

Writing this book has been an anchor through the coronavirus pandemic for me. For the first two months of lockdown or social distancing I have resisted productivity narratives and let myself cry on the floor while eating my way through all my waves of feelings, which was exactly what I needed. The third month began with a beautiful full moon in Scorpio and a feeling of being a little more settled in this new reality, so I returned to my writing practice.

Every morning my puppy wakes me up no later than 6 am. I feed my dogs, brush my teeth, put some clothes on and head to the beach down the road. Living in a village on the East Coast of Scotland means we still have easy access to natural beauty, for which I am so grateful. We play for a bit, Ernie chases some birds and chews a few sticks and then we return home. I shower, light a candle, make my favorite tea and then write a thousand words or more before I do anything else. Some days it's hard and I am tired, but most of the time it feels like a very soothing practice. I am thinking a lot about how I want to let this time change me and I know that we have to fall apart in order to be remade. When I pay attention I can see that in the midst of loss and injustice there is also a beautiful emergence of slowness, heightened creativity, and solidarity all around me. It makes me hope sincerely that life will never be the same after this, even if the chaos of change feels deeply unsettling.

As someone who is neurodivergent and purposefully weird, I am incredibly reluctant to accept change and am often bewildered by the human experience. Rituals have therefore become an invaluable source of support for me, especially right now. I feel that rituals are a way for our souls to catch up with what is happening around us and are also a way to work with our intentions and desires in meaningful ways.

I'm wondering how we can stop participating in capitalism for good, beyond the temporary closure of our shopping malls due to the pandemic. I also want to know how we as white people can move from short lived reactions to police violence against black people that has always been there to working towards a radical, sustained long term transformation of our justice and community safety systems. It's easier to see capitalism and other systems of oppression as an *other*, something outside of myself that I have nothing to do with. But I know, like we probably all do on some level, that I have chosen to participate in the wrong kinds of rituals for a long time. This time of grief, chaos, and solitude is giving us so much to think about. It makes me feel hopeful and excited when people say they don't want to go back to "normal," even though I know we don't actually have a solid plan for anything else yet. Maybe this is a crucial moment. It certainly is a crucial time to act around climate change as we only have a small window of time left to avoid warming beyond a level that would cause unthinkable catastrophes in our lifetimes. Spelling out the idea of terrible things happening *in my lifetime* I am noticing a sense of urgency that I wouldn't feel if I was writing about some kind of lifetime for some kind of future generation. I really think that is telling us a lot about how disconnected we've become from this cycle of life that we do actually belong to. I can see in myself that this cognitive dissonance is mirrored in the kinds of rituals I've committed to in the past, like pressing a button and expecting something made of plastic to arrive at my door the next day. And I know this has to stop.

2020 is a wild year. I've never experienced this much intensity and contrast in such a condensed period of time. I'm sleeping much more than usual to try to process as best as I can. I am drawing on seen and unseen resources. On one hand, there are all these brutal losses of people, spaces, relationships, and stability. And then the rage from knowing that a lot of it could have been avoided. Then there are bits of hope because suddenly things we've always wanted are possible. Mutual aid networks have popped up everywhere, more people can finally work from home (yet working class people are disproportionately affected by being sent back to work), and we're slowing all the way down. We're forced to think about how unsustainable our lives really have been or, more simply, how much joy and connection we've really allowed ourselves to feel so far. For me, staying present without being crushed by the chaos of this moment is the biggest challenge.

After the brutal murder of George Floyd, another unarmed black man at the hands of a white police officer, more people are willing to admit that the police aren't actually protecting our communities, especially not marginalised ones. We need new ways of finding justice and we finally need to confront the structural racism that's deeply ingrained in all elements of society. There is no more looking away and there is also no excuse for the ways we have been complacent and ignorant in the past. It's a wake up call that has always been there, it has just gotten much louder.

How can we sustain this momentum in our movements? How can we make sure we're not becoming complicit in our oppression by burning ourselves out? How can we create conditions that ensure we're able to show up for what we believe in in the long run and as best as we can?

I have taught ritual practices online for a few years now and really love the gentleness of small, mostly body based practices that as a whole and over time add up to something that feels very nourishing and luminous. It helps a bit and that really matters to me.

While I have been making rituals all my life I'm also writing this as someone with very little experience of highly formalised group ritual. I am pretty socially awkward and find large groups difficult, so these kinds of things often haven't felt accessible to me. I have trained in a few different bodywork modalities, was lucky to learn about ritual practice and folk magic from some wonderful experiential teachers and studied creative writing as well as collaborative media practices for social change, so those are the strands I am weaving together here. This book is not a complete history of ritual across time and cultures, but a snapshot of one human at one point in time asking questions about the world and how to live in it. There are many cultures that have much older, larger and more creative bodies of work around ritual practice than I have as a white person and I honour them while also trying my best to stay in my own lane.

Having time and space to write this book feels like a huge blessing right now, even if I also feel a bit shy about it. When I remember some of the poetry I published in my early and mid twenties I cringe and wish I could take it back. I am trying not to think about it too much, because I know the self-consciousness stops me in my tracks. Having built two businesses in parts through social media over the past five years I also know how fast things can move and how quickly our language and thinking can develop. And in a way I do hope that this book will feel dated ten years from now too. I hope that my practice will have deepened, that it has more nuance and that we collectively have healed and integrated some of what is happening in 2020. So in moments when I am feeling hesitant to share these mostly very personal thoughts I remind myself that it's okay for them to also have their own lifecycle and to eventually be recycled, literally and metaphorically.

On the other hand I do think that rituals can have a timelessness to them and that they have something to offer to anyone at any time with whatever is available. My hope is that in reading *Rituals* you'll find some solace, some grounding and some inspiration for your own rituals and resistance. I also hope that this book will offer you a framework to explore a practice of resilience at this time and maybe even a spirituality of your own understanding. I think that finding our own truths and staying connected to something beyond our own lives is a very important skill that will support all of us in better navigating whatever happens next.

It's my intention to make the practices I am sharing in this book as accessible as possible while being culturally sensitive and honouring my teachers. I won't make assumptions about who you are in this book, about what you are able to do or about what you have access to. There will also be no gendered language, and while trauma will be briefly mentioned, there won't be any graphic details. You are welcome to take from this what feels good and then leave the rest.

Traditionally, rituals have three parts to them: separation from ordinary life; the middle part, which I like to think of as a magical, liminal space; and then the integration or returning home part. In the smallest sense this could mean intending a moment of quiet from a busy day (separation), lighting a candle and sitting with it (liminal space) and then blowing it out to go to bed a little calmer (integration), but of course there are also countless beautiful ways in which this rhythm can play out in larger poetic and mysterious ways.

If you apply this framework to life you might find that there have been times in which you have been separated from something familiar against your will and that this separation threw you into a kind of liminal space, regardless of whether you wanted to be there or not. You might also see a pattern of return, moments in which you can recognise that the break up, the job loss or the decline of health or ability did teach you something as you made your way back home and found ways to integrate this experience.

It feels important to say that meaning making should never be forced. I get so frustrated when folks who experience deep personal hardship and/or systemic oppression get told that it all happens for a reason, that we should just "up our frequency." This is not what I am saying at all. In fact, I hope that rituals can help us find a language for the systemic injustice we are seeing and experiencing without trapping us in a place of victimhood. Finding meaning has to come naturally, on its own terms. And it does not negate injustice. We all may or may not find some silver lining in harm we've experienced, but to bypass the rage, sadness and grief that we have to move through is just toxic positivity. We all may also use the moments of solitude we're creating in ritual to better understand the situations in which we have caused harm and to find ways to do better moving forward.

It wont work to leave parts of ourselves behind if we want to arrive in a place of integration and wholeness.

In my experience, practicing this non-linear, sometimes confusing and unpredictable pattern of separation/liminality/integration in small ways, such as in our own homes, bodies, and communities, will help us navigate the bigger waves of change, too. I am wondering what it will feel like to look back at 2020 ten years from now. I wonder what we will have learned from this and if we will have managed to hold on to some of the good bits—the slowness, the possibility for re-imagination, the solidarity.

To me grief tending is an important part of this work, as is pleasure seeking. It is hard to be certain of anything right now, but I am certain that we will need skills in these areas to move through the next few years and beyond.

As you explore the following chapters please let them be an invitation for kindness with yourself and others. Let's be culturally sensitive and mindful of our own privileges, let's share the resources we have as freely as we can, let's be aware of the violent history and presence of colonialism, capitalism, and other forms of oppression. This will be an imperfect process, but refusing to engage in this very important work would leave our practices feeling hollow and superficial.

This book begins with a long chapter on the elements of ritual followed by a chapter with more specific ritual ideas. I close with a chapter on developing a supportive regular practice to lean into. You can start at the very beginning or you can dip in and out of chapters as and when they speak to you. I also like the practice of book divination: think of a question or of a situation you need support around (if in doubt let it be just the present moment) and then close your eyes and let your fingers run through the pages until you feel like you want to stop. Then open the page and see what you'll find.

Thank you for reading my book. I've done my best to step out of the way and just write what I thought needed to be written, but I can tell that my brain is operating slightly differently at this time and I'm hoping that my book's imperfection will encourage you to make your own imperfect things.

In love & solidarity,

Yarrow

PART I

ELEMENTS OF RITUAL

In this chapter I am sharing some general elements of ritual practice that are working well for me. This is by no means a comprehensive list as there is always more to discover and work with. As I said, I'm a big fan of simplicity and will usually combine just one or two elements into a soft, doable ritual.

I hope the following pages might give you some ideas to help you in creating your own ritual practice or at least the joy of hearing a new perspective if you already have one. This chapter is by far the largest in the book because I think it's much more fun to have a readily available toolbox of things to play with, rather than a long catalogue of prescriptive rituals that might not feel totally right for you.

I found over the years that making notes about my experiments has really helped me feel more confident and intuitive in the way I work with these elements. If that idea feels exciting, I invite you to keep a journal just for your ritual ideas and reflections.

That way you can note your observations, collect ideas, and create your own framework for ritual practice that is perfect for your circumstances and desires.

Enchantment

To me enchantment is a lifeline. It's going into the forest to snotty cry during a pandemic and leaning against a tree for cuddles. It's knowing that even though borders are closed, I can still let my mind travel freely. It's also remembering that I am not separate from anything and that I can feel belonging, even when my human relationships are complicated and sometimes overwhelming.

Ever since I was little, imagination and storytelling have been important playgrounds to experiment and grow within. Especially right now I am sensing that time can stretch out and contract in so many ways depending on where my mind wanders. Seeing physical reality and imagination as a binary doesn't make sense to me when really everything we have created was once a dream. I'm thinking about folk tales and how much they've shaped my sense of what is possible, of my identity as well as my moral compass. I'm also thinking about how myths often travel from the lips of our grandmothers to our children's ears, existing in both the past and the future as a bridge between collective realities.

My hope is that a sense of enchantment feeds our capacity for radical imagination so that we can reach for something far beyond capitalism, white supremacy, and patriarchy. I am also hopeful that it will help us untangle the cognitive dissonance we're sometimes experiencing, that the lack of coherence between our values and actions will be illuminated by ritual.

I think daydreaming is a practice of enchantment. It requires comfort with solitude and boredom as well as good rest. It lets us drop below the surface of intellectual exploration, deeper into the places of wonder and possibility, as if we were diving into a lake. Isn't it true for most of us that our best ideas come in the shower or while walking or cycling? This makes sense to me because in those moments the gentle, repetitive movement is rocking my nervous system into a relaxed, receptive state. One in which I don't have to hold it all in my brain, where I can let my animal body speak.

Yesterday I spent a soft Sunday reading in bed and playing in the garden with Ernie the puppy. I watched him and realized how completely immersed in the experience of being a puppy he is at all times. How he sniffs and barks and rolls around with a kind of presence that is often lost to humans. When I opened my laptop he came closer and put his head on the keyboard asking why I wasn't playing. There isn't really any future tripping or thinking about past regrets on his mind. He is just there smelling things, appreciating them for what they are in all their ordinary magic while having a great time. He knows enchantment. It makes me want to ask how I can be fully present with the experience of being a human in a global pandemic, through times of collapse. What is it like to be present to disaster and also to pleasure?

In the last few weeks I have often gone into the forest to rest and ask what to do. It's a great place to think because it's quiet yet full of bird song, it's fully colour coordinated in beautiful shades of green and it changes dramatically each week, especially in spring. After just a few weeks of warmer temperatures the ground is covered in bluebells, wild garlic and fern. The forest models collaboration, solidarity, and abundance to me and everyone who cares to visit. It makes me wonder how many more years or generations we'll keep banging our heads against the wall of endless linear growth before we start radically and fairly redistributing our wealth. Yesterday when I called my dogs back and said goodbye to the trees to walk back home the questions that came to me where

Have I really tried sharing power?

Am I redistributing my own wealth where it is in abundance?

Are we really trying this in our homes, in our romantic relationships?

In what ways have we tried starting where the stakes are the highest? What have we learned from that? What is needed to succeed?

What can we do to return our power back home, to call it back from places where it's being hoarded by billionaires?

How can we rest our bodies in spaces where we can speak our truth and carry the responsibility of our actions?

And it was like the forest whispered

Let it all come to you.

Go back to your species and try again.

Ritual & mental health

I have no doubt that rituals are good for my mental health on so many levels and want to name just a few of the ways in which they make my life better here:

They offer a space to slow down and be present with my feelings.

They create deeper connections with others.

They allow me to be creative and express myself in simple, doable ways.

They give my life a sense of rhythm and pace.

They strengthen my sense of belonging.

They help me to make space for grief when needed.

They invite me to spend more time outside.

I'm excited about Silvia Federici's writing about re-enchantment and the commons and am curious about the ways in which shared ritual helps us build and strengthen spiritual commons outside of capitalist enclosure.

We have so many deeply ingrained rituals already - the way we check our phones dozens of times a day, the ritual of turning Netflix on and checking out, brushing our teeth, how we cook our dinners and sit down to eat.

I think there is also an aspect of stability that feels very important to me. For example, when I am doing my daily morning pages what I am telling my subconscious mind is that my thoughts and experiences matter, that they are worth time and paper for exploration. In a chaotic world I am becoming reliable to myself and I create supportive structures that maybe aren't as easily accessible elsewhere.

I don't think that our own ritual practice can or should replace therapy or medical interventions, of course. But I think they can complement other approaches and give us more of the intimacy and slowness we are often missing. Sometimes creating our own rituals around beginning a new treatment or taking pills in the morning for example can make us feel more engaged and intentional in the process of healing, which is so beautiful.

Life under capitalism can feel disorienting and forces us to fall in line with things that for many of us are not a natural way to be. Dreading Mondays because our work is exhausting is not normal or necessary. Growing up in educational systems that pit us against each other and instill shame and competition is not normal or necessary. Living in constant fear of not being able to meet our basic needs for shelter, food, clean air and water as well as a sense of belonging is not normal or necessary. Believing that there is only one way to "be completed" by another person who is meant to meet all our needs and expectations is not normal or necessary.

But it's hard to step away from these things and to co-create something different. It's hard to always be questioning, to be hypervigilant, to often expect the worst and still be creative. I light up when I see rituals providing just a little more energy and comfort and sustenance for everything that we are already doing to resist and everything that is yet to come.

Cultural Appropriation

To me healing is always political. I don't think that we can separate what we are doing in our own homes and bodies from the power structures we are living within. As white people we have a responsibility to look at our privileges and dismantle white supremacy. Whitewashing, commercialisation and appropriation have become big problems in the spiritual industries, which is something we need to urgently address. Many of us are seeking traditions and practices outside of our own culture to fill the spiritual emptiness we're feeling, which is harmful. I know I have done this and I want to make sure I won't do it again.

Our ritual making, enchantment feeling and dreaming can't continue to happen at the cost of folks of colour. If we think we are entitled to claim, appropriate, and commercialise spiritual practices from people who have long been and still are being punished for honouring these practices we are replicating the very same colonial thinking that has already caused so much trauma and violence. Referring to your "spirit animal" or offering sweat lodges with little or no understanding of the cultural context of these traditions for example isn't cute, it's violent.

It is important that we are always seeking to be in reciprocity, which of course can mean different things at different times. We have to listen deeply, name, pay and honour our teachers and seek permission where appropriate. We also have to operate with great care and ask ourselves hard questions about the integrity of our work. When we pause to think about it, we can see that these are not actually big things to ask of ourselves at all. Being able to sit with the discomfort of our history and privilege should be something we invite as a vital part of ritual practice and everything else in our lives.

I have made many mistakes in this area myself. About ten years ago I trained as a yoga teacher without really contextualising myself as a white person in an industry that benefits from the commercialisation of ancient practices for example. My intentions were good - I wanted to teach donation based, body positive yoga classes in queer communities. I saw a need and a possibility to offer something helpful. But sometimes good intentions aren't good enough. Yoga belongs to a culture that has experienced an enormous amount of colonial violence, so who are we to water it down, package it up, and sell it at costs that often exclude those who might need the practice the most? What are we really giving in fair exchange for these ancient teachings we have received and how are we honouring these lineages? What does it mean when we pose on instagram with bindis to get likes, while people of colour will experience discrimination for wearing them at a job interview? I am sorry for the ways in which I have been a part of that and I'm grateful for and indebted to the educators of colour who are sharing what they know with me.

All of us are being invited to make active listening, reciprocity, and a willingness to work with discomfort and privilege a priority. At the end of the book you'll find some books that might help you explore what this could look like for you.

Reciprocity

I started working when I was eleven. I looked after middle class kids, sold ice cream, washed hair, and filed papers after school. And then I went to H&M to buy fast fashion items, things that now still have hundreds of years in a landfill until they will finally decompose. I remember the dopamine high from buying them and having something new to wear and also the fast pace with which this pleasure wore off. I didn't know much about the sustainability of different materials and hardly ever thought much about diet culture, western beauty standards or self-image issues. I feel regret about how I spent my time and energy then, even though I know that I just wanted to belong and feel good about myself.

The truth is that there was no reciprocity.

I was taken from and also have taken from the Earth, from underpaid garment workers, from natural resources. I took more than I really needed without a second thought. As soon as I was able to make my own money I assumed my place within the great cycle of mindless consumerism.

It took me a surprisingly long time to notice how shit it is to not be in healthy, mutual exchange with everything and everyone I am in relationship with. It feels precarious and hollow, like a very old Easter egg that could collapse into itself any second. Desire for belonging can be a powerful political instrument and it's hard, really hard to notice how much we're willing to sacrifice to be able to buy the latest things. The headspace to think about these things is a privilege not many single mothers who are just trying to put food on the table have.

Reciprocity doesn't mean that we always have to give back exactly the amount that we receive, that would be impossible. Reciprocity can be fluid, adaptable, open and kind. It can make space for times of great need, for different ideas and abilities, for movement and for questions. I think that all it requires to exist is an openness and a willingness to be of service and to share resources freely.

When I am thinking about what reciprocity might mean in ritual practice I am thinking about sharing ideas and practices widely where appropriate and culturally sensitive. I am also thinking about bringing more clarity to what it is that we are taking to be part of our practice and from whom. There might be beeswax from honeybees, tarot cards made from trees, crystals mined from places we've never been to. It can be okay to have these things, but I think most of us can spend more time appreciating their origin, exploring what local and regenerative alternatives might be available and giving thanks while paying fairly for what we do take.

Reciprocity also comes to mind when I am thinking about the perceived binary of self- and community care. Self-care has become a huge industry in the last few years - as I write this in spring 2020 there are more than 27 million posts on the selfcare hashtag on instagram for example. What was once a radical concept that black, feminist authors such as Audre Lorde wrote about has been whitewashed, appropriated, commercialised, and watered down. More recently we've started to write and talk about what community care means and how it's related to self-care—as if that's a new idea—when of course the necessity of community care has been vital and clear to marginalised and indigenous communities forever. I do think that for many of us our emotional and physical resources are so depleted that we have to start with small, doable things at home, in our own bodies. That might be a bubble bath or simply switching our phones off more often, but those things in themselves, without a community context, will never be enough if we want to feel belonging as a part of something larger than ourselves.

Reciprocity is also a practice of place making. When I am in reciprocity I can't see myself as separate from and entitled to the resources and beauty of places. I'm clear that it's not okay to just show up and take what I want because I am paying a marginal price for it, one that is nowhere near fair or negotiated in a liberated exchange. Instead, I am examining the consequences of my actions and finding ways of being in a mutually beneficial relationship with everything around me. With that I might find a sense of belonging and a space to grow roots.

A ritual practice might help me see the bigger picture of what I am doing and lead me towards a more gentle way of traveling through space.

Accessibility

Once we understand that a felt sense of interconnectedness is an integral part of enchantment, it's easy to see why it is important that our ritual practice is accessible to ourselves and everyone we are sharing them with. And of course there is no fixed formula for accessibility, it can mean a lot of different things at different times. For some people, physical accessibility might be the most important thing, for others financial accessibility might matter. And for some other people, having a clear outline on what is planned might be needed to make a good decision on whether or not they want to go.

I definitely fall into the last category and need to be able to do some planning before I'm participating in a group situation. Obviously I can't know what someone else might be needing without intentional and active listening on my part. Beyond asking kind and open questions I think we also have to cultivate communities in which it's okay to have needs and to voice them while also developing communication skills that are empowering and liberatory.

In this book I am trying to offer practices that are financially affordable, that don't deplete ecological resources, and that can be done with relatively little energy in different kinds of settings. I think in that way creativity is also an important part of accessibility—making space for things to be different than expected, to work with whatever time and resources we actually have available.

When I started getting interested in ritual practices I sometimes experienced the ideas I encountered as too rigid, complicated or prescriptive. I can obviously see the value in having a shared formal practice within a community, but for myself I decided to prioritise a gentle, easy kind of consistency. Being able to do small things almost every day rather than big things occasionally feels good. I want a stable, nourishing sense of enchantment and comfort in my life and I find big groups of people very hard. It's totally okay to feel differently of course, you do you and make this work your own.

Grounding & Protection

Knowing how to stay grounded and protected is of course really important. I don't think there is any reason to be scared or to overcomplicate things, but of course rituals, like many other things, can bring up difficult emotions or challenging memories. It is always good to know what brings you comfort in life and to have some of those things handy when you go into your ritual practice.

I would like to share a few questions that you can journal on which might point you towards the things that make you feel grounded and protected:

- What do I intuitively reach for when I feel upset? Does this feel like a good coping mechanism to me at this time or do I want to explore other options?
- What makes me feel safer in my home and my body? Are there are boundaries I want to draw around my ritual practice (for example telling housemates not to disturb me, turning my phone off or spending a specific evening each week alone to care for myself)?
- Are there any themes or subjects that feel upsetting to me at the moment so that they should be avoided in my practice?

I'll share a bit about what grounding and safety means to me too, bearing in mind that these things are often changing. To me feeling grounded means to be in my body most of the time and to feel some sense of solid connection to the space I'm in as well as the passing of time. I feel grounded on my daily walks, connecting with my local landscapes, seeing things grow and looking at the waves. I also feel grounded when I fall asleep under my weighted blanket in a pile with my two dogs or when I tend to my home and light candles. When I am grounded I know my place in the world and have a sense of belonging and connection. Self-awareness also feels like an important aspect of grounding to me—when I am grounded I am listening to my body and I know my limits. I don't overstretch my resources and am able to say no when I need to. Self-awareness to me isn't just about understanding my own actions, desires and traits, it's also about body literacy, about being able to be present with sensations, shifts of energy or patterns and understanding my nervous system as well as everything else that is part of my being.

Feelings of safety can be more complicated for me, but there are still many things I find helpful, even if I don't usually experience a "perfect" sense of safety. Slowness is a key piece for me—giving myself a bit of time to feel things out, not rushing through decisions and making time to know and then articulate what I want and need. Preparation is another key part in my experience, the more I know about a new situation, the safer I will feel in it. I'm trying to be intentional with the kinds of spaces, people and ideas I engage with and to always deepen my trust in my own intuition as best as I can.

Altars

Altars are sometimes also called shrines and generally speaking they are spaces we create for our spiritual practice. I love them because they give me a focal point and a way to draw my attention to my practices as well as a space to be creative and shift things throughout the seasons.

As with most things I find simplicity to be really attractive for my altars and I try to not stuff them with too many things. An altar can be as simple as a tea light on your window sill with a special stone that you found. Other elements that might feel nice are tarot cards that you've drawn and want to work with for longer, found objects like leafs or rocks, letters, drawings, photos or herbal potions.

Tending to my alters - dusting them off, rearranging the items on them and just making sure they feel cared for is really important to me. If you would like to make one for yourself really all you need is a nice corner somewhere quiet that you can fill with a few special objects and some intention. It can reflect your desires, something you want to draw attention to or simply be a place of stillness.

My current main altar is a corner of my bedroom in which a simple white box is surrounded by various linen and velvet cushions in rose colours. There are weavings on the wall, pictures of a snake and a bear and then a candle and a stone. The morning sun washes the space in warmth and sometimes me and the dogs just hang out there and cuddle after I say my prayers or draw my cards.

When I lived in that teeny tiny house in Brighton, a space that was so small it did not fit a normal sofa let alone a full sized desk, I made my altar under the stairs that led up to the loft bed. An old microwave was covered with white fabric and decorated with pictures and dried rose petals. I knew it was not the size of the space of the price of the decorations that mattered, but the time that I allowed myself to just sit there, thinking of nothing in particular while letting my body rest.

Working with the elements

I find elemental work incredibly helpful in bringing balance to any situation and also in getting to know a local landscape with its beauty and unique traits. Generally speaking I am referring to earth, water, fire and air when I speak about elements, but I want to name that this is a European way of looking at it and that there are different elemental frameworks in other cultures across the world.

I find it interesting to ask myself which element is most present in any given situation that I am working with and also to explore what my association with those elements are. What makes a situation earthy? What kind of person is watery?

I am a water sign in Western astrology and it does feel like my favorite element, I feel at home swimming in the sea. I think of water as free, deep, healing, fluid and relational. The words that come to mind when I think about earth are nourishing, rich, steady, grounded and cozy while fire makes me think about warmth, creativity, sexuality, destruction and expansion and air makes me think about movement, ideas, the sky, communication and change.

Many people enjoy working with elements in correspondence to the four directions of the wheel of the year, meaning that the East represents Air, the South represents Fire, the West represents Water and the North represents Earth. In that way you can create rituals in which you bring in something representing each element in one corner or direction, for example candles, cups of water, feathers, rocks, pieces of wood or plants.

Another way of doing elemental work is to invite in an element or two that feels particularly helpful for something you are trying to do. If you are starting or revisiting a creative project for example you could have a little candle ceremony that brings a lot of warmth and light to your work. You could write about your intention surrounded by candle light and light a candle every time you engage with the project.

If you are going through a period of change it might be nice to work with air to facilitate a smooth transition. I love standing outside in a storm or opening all my windows to feel the force and energy and imagining it carrying away any heaviness or stuckness in my life. On the other hand I also feel that with how digital and fast paced our lives have become, most situations benefit from more earthy grounding and a solid sense of orientation in time and space.

All this to say that I think the elements are a beautiful and easy way to play, work with symbolism, explore meaning and subconscious desires or ideas and feel more connected to the places we inhabit.

Ancestors

All of us have ancestors who had a reciprocal, loving relationship with the Earth and creative ritual practices, even if our more recent ancestors might have had different lived experiences. Connecting with the people we come from isn't always easy for all kinds of reasons. Some of us simply don't know them, some of us are having a hard time tracing our lineages across the planet, some of us will be heartbroken to learn about the suffering the people who came before them have endured and some of us will find that our ancestors have been complicit in brutal systems of oppression. Folks with European backgrounds, including myself, need to confront the shameful and violent histories of our colonising ancestors and work to dismantle white supremacy, which I believe should be a central part of our ritual practice.

We can remember that while we carry ancestral burdens, we also carry ancestral blessings. Especially right now I am exploring how my ancestors have survived pandemics and famines, how they dealt with displacement and trauma. I want to know what made them strong and adaptable and what gave them hope. There is a story of my grandmother for example, who made the long overland journey from Ukraine to Northern Germany towards the end of the second world war by hiding in forests and reading the night sky. She was still a young child and traveled alone with my great grandmother. They were incredibly lucky to have left just before the rest of the village was brought to Siberia. For some reason these two women survived on very little food and managed to believe that to keep walking was worth it, that there was something beyond this that they could not yet touch, that was waiting for them on the other side. My grandmother went on to fall in love, start a family, build a house, and do work in her community.

What might a connection to your ancestors look like in your own ritual practice? Do you have relationships with living or recently dead ancestors that feel heavy or difficult that maybe you'd prefer not to make part of your exploration? It's good to have boundaries and it's okay to start small where you are. If this feels good, orient yourself towards your well ancestors, those you can relate to with ease and trust. Learning about their stories, about the things that made them strong and then bringing those things into your own life might be a beautiful way to deepen your ritual work. Every one of us has ancestors in their bloodline who have been creative and resilient, who loved well, and who have wisdom to share. Maybe connecting with them can help us to make sure we won't repeat the mistakes they've made.

Ancestral remembrance doesn't have to be boring or heavy. You can learn about the stories your people carried across time and space, make your grandmother's favorite dishes or learn about crafts, traditions or beliefs your ancestors held dear. I know not all of us have access to this information while others have only memories that are painful to hold. If this feels true for you it might be good to remember that we are always free to start new traditions and to tell different stories. We can even question the very concept of family in order to create a new sense of kinship with the world.

In addition to exploring our families and ancestors we can also remember that we come from plants and stones and stars, all of which have been here long before humans walked on Earth. Plants have grown and shape shifted on this planet even before there were animals, and stones have been here even longer than that. Especially when what is present right now feels overwhelming and difficult, I like to lean into the timelessness of the non-human world. Asking myself how a mountain might experience my lifetime really as a blink of an eye makes me feel small in a good way. It puts things into perspective and it helps me remember that I am a child of the wilderness as much as I am my parent's child.

Death awareness

I've lived most of my life not really present to the fact that I'll die one day. Until last year I did not have an advance directive or an end of life plan. I hadn't thought about my choices and what I would want at my death bed or about how I would leave things behind. For most of us death feels so far away and if we're lucky it is.

The death midwife training I did in 2019 really opened my eyes to how beautiful it can be to live with an embodied understanding of impermanence. Whatever it is that sucks isn't going to be here forever. Whatever it is that I'm in love with also isn't going to be here forever. It felt scary at first, to do things like writing goodbye letters and making decisions about being resuscitated or not, but ultimately it is really peaceful to have done that. I think of our ability to think and talk about death as a muscle we can build and I am really grateful for the natural death and death positivity movements for gently but powerfully raising my awareness of things that are really just a normal part of life.

I don't have a clear cut belief about what happens after we die and I am pretty okay with that. There is a lot I don't know. I guess it's human nature to seek proof and in this case there are many limitations around what we can experience about death before our time comes. My hunch is that death isn't the absolute and finite end we sometimes make it to be, but I don't know what else it is. I do know that we live through memories, that our actions are creating tiny ripple effects for eternity, and that we may well return in some way.

I'm trying to hold death awareness tenderly in my ritual practice. It shows up in the form of grief tending, in accepting winter and things dying down and in just naming the truth of death occasionally. I like the way fire can turn a letter I wrote about something I want to end to ashes and how I can add that to compost as a symbol of my trust in the life cycle of things.

Right now I am of course also thinking about how we can bring death to the things that got us to this place of mass extinction and violent injustice. I'm sensing the connection between death avoidance and the linear growth capitalism both wants and needs to survive. I'm also interested in how this relates to the way we value youth and pay so much money to avoid signs of ageing, how we worship summer and external energy. There is something scary and very uncertain about confronting the end of things if we have so little practice in being intimate with death and good grief. I guess that is showing up in how hard we are finding it to let go of the unsustainable ways in which we've been living right now.

If you're interested in exploring death awareness you'll find some book recommendations at the end of this book and there are also a few simple yet powerful questions that I think we all benefit from working with:

- How would I like to die?
- What would I regret not doing before I die?
- What is my belief about what happens after death?
- How do I feel grief?

At this time all of us have a chance to grieve losing the way things were. While our experiences of the pandemic will be wildly different depending on our backgrounds, experiences, and the things we have access to, we all have lost a sense of certainty. All of us are no longer able to carry on as if nothing happened. I think it's okay and understandable to grieve the loss of things we know deep down weren't good for us anyway. We might hate the commute to work but still feel sad about being stuck at home. We might enjoy the new slowness of life and still miss the excitement of a packed weekend filled with exploration and socialising. Whatever comes next has to be built on compassion for ourselves and others as well as strong grief literacy, otherwise I really believe we will run into the same walls, pandemics, and acts of violence over and over again.

Now that I have all this solitude I want to ask myself, what is a good death? What will I write about in my final weeks and months? Many things in the past twelve months opened my eyes to a very simple yet often forgotten fact of life: we are all going to die.

Activism & Justice

I don't think there is a part of life that isn't political and I think that rituals can be a good way to make our activism more sustainable and regenerative. Anger is beautiful and sadness is a great access point to change, especially when we have practices that help us to be present to and communicate these feelings. There doesn't need to be a binary between activism and spirituality either -- maybe showing up for a mutual aid group or writing letters to prisoners is your ritual and maybe it is also your activism.

One of the first things that come to mind when I think of ritual as activism is to go out and pick up litter if that's possible. I do it occasionally and it's just so sweet in its simplicity. We can all show gratitude for the spaces we get to inhabit and make them more enjoyable for everyone we share them with, including birds and insects and plants. This is also a practice that helps me through times in which I find organising with groups of people too difficult and overwhelming or times in which meeting with local groups simply isn't always possible, like right now during the pandemic.

To develop your own understanding of ritual as activism or activism as ritual it might be illuminating to ask yourself what causes you are feeling devoted to right now and what you're able to give to them. I like the word devotion in this context because it feels so different from duty or peer pressure or reactivity. The things I am devoted to are aligned with all parts of myself, with my political ideas, my identities, and with what's in my heart of hearts.

Another thing you can ask yourself is in what ways the causes you're excited about are already utilising ritual, what these rituals look like and what other rituals might be supportive. I love the ritual of growing food for each other, or medicine making, of chanting together, of shared art making and writing and expressing fear, rage and frustration in togetherness. Getting ready for protest together, thinking about strategies to keep each other safe and being creative and effective can also be a ritual. It's just as important to find practices for outward expression of political work as it is to find quieter, more internal rituals to reflect, regroup, and recharge.

Rituals with others

I love being in ritual with small groups or just one other person, but should probably say that I do most of my rituals by myself. I think rituals can be a great way to get to know people in a new and deeper way and to make special memories together. Maybe there is also a soothing element in having a planned, structured activity together instead of the usual open catch up.

It's good to spend more time checking in on what everyone involved is hoping to get from a ritual and to find out where people fall on the spectrum of highly formalised ceremony to experiential, improvised ritual. Many of the ideas I am sharing in this book can easily be shared with other people and of course there are many creative ways in which you can make them your own or weave them together the ritual ideas and experiences of other folks.

Are you part of a spiritual community? If the answer is no, would you like to be part of one? How are you feeling about joining a group or starting a new one with people you know? I love the idea of non-hierarchical communities or practice, but I'm also very aware of their complexity. We all bring such different things into this work and it can be hard and time consuming to find a way of being together that feels good and is fair for everyone involved. I have done this and I will do this again because I believe it is worth it. At the same time, I am also allowing myself time and space to lean into solitude and to strengthen my own practices that can exist independently from whatever else is happening around me.

Maybe our intuitive ways of discerning between the need to be alone and the need to be together is another muscle we can grow over time. It takes self-awareness, good boundaries and of course access to a community that allows us to be fully ourselves in exchange and dialogue with other people. These things aren't always available, which is why I think it's so important that we practice patience with each other.

Sometimes I'm noticing in myself that I do wish for leadership and I am trying to be very careful with that desire. Having grown up the way we have there might be a sense of comfort in seeking situations in which we're being "led" or told what to do without needing to do all the hard work of exploration, creation and discernment ourselves, but obviously there are very real dangers in handing our power over in that way. In some small ways I'm seeing this reflected on social media right now -- we do seem to value the opinions of people that have large followings more than others, and we do seem to think that something we have said matters more when we have received many likes.

Group work can be a great space to be together but also to come closer to ourselves through experimentation in relationships. It's an invitation to sit with the complexity and discomfort of truly sharing power and negotiating processes in ways that are liberating for everyone involved.

Working with the moon

Mhhh, I love the moon, I appreciate the moon, I cannot imagine my life without the moon.

Time can often fly by fast under capitalism when we focus so much on endless expansion and productivity. The moon feels like a steady and magical reminder to go slow, to track time differently, and to trust the cyclical ebb and flow of things.

The moon is not linear and neither am I.

Working with the moon doesn't have to be all "out there," though of course it can be as far gone with the fairies as you'd like it to be (I have always loved this expression and wondered why it could be a bad thing, who wouldn't want to be gone with the fairies instead of being at a boring job?).

Tracking your energy levels and mood alongside the moon (and your hormonal cycle if you have one) can be a beautiful way to pay loving attention to yourself and your needs for example. This could be as simple as dedicating the last few pages of your journal just to tracking and to draw up a simple chart that lists the date, the phase of the moon and then a little note on how you were feeling. You could invent little symbols for different moods or just track your energy level or enthusiasm for life on a scale from one to ten. If you do this for three months you might be able to see patterns emerging and you could then use these patterns to set yourself up for self-care in future cycles as you're even better able to anticipate your needs.

It can also be interesting to think and write about your associations with different phases of the moon or to look up under which moon phase you were born. Do you have a favorite moon phase? Maybe you love the fullness and bright light of the full moon or appreciate the new beginning and sense of starting over that the new moon brings? There are so many other aspects of the moon that are exciting too - the way the waning moon reminds us to let go, the shadowy comfort and stillness of the dark moon, the way the waxing moon can feel like spring and growth and ripening.

Intentions & Affirmations

Affirmations were not always an easy love for me. Sometimes I felt that I was just plastering the repetition of something that doesn't actually feel true for me over something that was pretty painful. I really find that it doesn't help to say something out loud if it doesn't feel true in my body. Yes, I guess to some extent we can fake it till we make it, but maybe there is also magic in talking about uncomfortable truths more often.

These days I am making small, heartfelt declarations a part of my practice. When I had really amazing sex for the first time after a period of recovery from an assault, I embroidered "pleasure is possible" on a piece of linen. I also love making labels for my herbal potions and call them things like "all that you are is all that you need" or "queer resilience." I think if we keep our minds open and playful beautiful phrases to work with will come naturally.

I feel similar about intentions, to me they are such an important part of making sure my practice is grounded and embodied. But they have to feel true. Without an intention I risk going through the motions, making things feel stale and repetitive. When I allow myself small, doable intentions and keep returning to them, I can say "I'd like to feel softer today," "I want to bring some more magic to this relationship," or "I need to make a big decision here" and really mean it.

I also love asking "Why?" more often. Why do I do this? Why does it matter? Why do I want to change something? Why am I reaching for this thing? Why does this feel so good? I think in a small way there is something very radical in taking a moment of pause to ask because the not pausing, the racing ahead, the accepting popular narratives as truth is exactly what is getting us into deep shit over and over again.

A more indirect way in which I am working with affirmations is to be very discerning with the stories, images and media in general I am taking in. I left Facebook for good last year and also took a six month break from Instagram. It felt good to return in the midst of the panic to check out what my friends are eating, to see everyone's pets, and most importantly to be angry together, but I'm trying to be careful with what I am affirming to myself. Sometimes looking through my discovery feed is just affirming that there is a certain kind of body type that is better than others for example and that's not the message I want to send to my subconscious mind.

What I want to affirm to myself is that liberation is possible, that the truth is beautiful, and that creativity is always available.

Folk Herbalism

I love plants and I love being in reciprocal relationships with them. I am not always very good at it, but I am trying. I am reminding myself everyday that I could literally not live without plants, that I breathe in and out with them and that they provide the fuel I need to be in this body. I also honour plants as my ancestors because that is who they are. They have been around much longer than my species and they have seen and survived much more than I have.

I am so humbled by plants. I know that some of them benefit from co-evolution with humans, but it still always feels like they are being way more generous than we are. Trying to be kind and reciprocal feels like a momentous task sometimes, because how could I ever return what they are giving me?

So I am starting small with where I am at. I am trying to work with beings of abundance rather than to take what is scarce, overharvested and endangered. I work with the overflow of weeds, I remember that Dandelions are flowers too and that Nettles are profound magic. I am trying to keep it local rather than to have non-native species shipped around the world and I am making an effort to save seeds and to listen to what is needed.

If you are new to folk herbalism I am inviting you to get to know just a few plants really well. I love the expression to slow down to plant seed, what a great idea. Be with the seasons, grow roots locally if you can, be adaptive. And of course be respectful -- if you are on stolen land, listen to indigenous folks who have been stewarding the land for millenia. We are just this tiny blink of an eye in the cosmic unfolding of things. To work with plants is to better know one's place in the world.

I'll mention some plants in some of my ritual ideas, but you'll probably find it to be much more enjoyable to work with what is easily available. If I could tell my younger self anything I would say not to overthink this, to let it be intuitive. Maybe Hawthorn feels particularly protective to you or maybe you are in love with roses as heart medicine. That is so beautiful. Of course you also want to make sure you know about safe usage and any contraindications there may be.

If you have the means to do this it might be nice to start a small home apothecary as part of your ritual practice. There are many online resources to learn more about how to make herbal infusions, herbal oils or tinctures for example and once you get a sense of the basics you'll have this amazing way of making healing magic for yourself and those you love.

Journeying

Maybe "journeying" is a pretentious word that can mean anything, I'm not sure. I guess what I mean in this context is an intentional exploration of our inner landscapes, memories and fantasies through meditation and stillness.

There are many different ways to do journeywork and each tradition will have its own framework, but generally speaking it is a practice of gently (or forcefully, if that's your jam) altering our state of consciousness to let our minds travel to places we usually don't get to visit. This could be facilitated by meditation, drumming, dance, music, breathwork, and other things.

I'm writing this part of the book seven weeks into lockdown in Scotland, a time abundant in quiet and solitude, but without any possibility for travel. It has sometimes been difficult to be alone with my thoughts so much when phone conversations with loved ones, occasional client calls and online classes I've taken can never replace the intimacy and connection of real life hugs.

I am very much an introvert and really only need and desire very little outside stimulation, but those shared dinners, evening classes and bookshop tours I used to do each month now seem incredibly necessary and very precious. In their absence I've been thinking about how journeywork might meet some of those longings when I was dreaming myself back to past holidays, relationships, spectacular meals and good parties.

When I'm sitting down to connect with my book I might imagine readers making their favorite tea to drink while they read it or I could dream of a book cover or something else that helps me trust the future of this project. Another example is lying down in a pile of pillows with a partner to dream back to the time we met, to return to the wonder and excitement we've been feeling for each other and to think about how that still matters and is present right now.

I also like thinking about younger versions of ourselves - about moments that overwhelmed us at the time and to find small ways in which we can give ourselves and each other what we would have needed then now as a journey of mending our memories.

Throughout the book I'll share some of my own experiences with journeywork and it might be interesting to get to know your own mind in a new way as you read along and experiment with the practices I am offering. Before you begin I invite you to think about what grounding and safety mean to you in this context, which could look like many different things. Maybe you want to have a favorite snack ready in case you want to bring yourself out of an experience that brought difficult emotions up or maybe you know that a certain smell is always calming for you. If you feel unsure, spend some extra time with the questions I have recommended in the grounding section of this chapter and proceed with great care for yourself and your experiences.

Meditation

Meditation can be hard and meditation can be a great healer. Maybe a big part of the reason why many people struggle with meditation is that we usually think of it as absolutely silent sitting cross legged on the floor for ages, which often feels impossible to do for me. I've experimented lots over the years and now use an app to time myself and choose a guided meditation when I don't feel able to be in stillness with my own thoughts. I also don't pressure myself into sitting there longer than I can or to reach complete stillness in my mind. I use a meditation pillow that really works for my body and I get up if I've had enough. The moral of this section is just that you can make your own meditation rules and there are many things that might help you make this practice easier. When you find your sweet spot, meditation can be a great emotional comfort zone in your day and it can also be a nice way to go into a ritual space.

If you're into engaging with research you can have a look around to explore some of the studies that found numerous benefits in regular meditation or alternatively you can just keep a journal, make a start with small daily meditation and record how it is or isn't changing your moods and how you experience life.

Divination

Divination can be described as a process that is meant to invite guidance from something bigger than ourselves by utilising tools like the tarot, runes, or a pendulum. I guess to many people this seems controversial or weird, but I think it really depends on how you look at it, how it makes sense in your body, and how you take responsibility for your own interpretation of things.

I don't think that you necessarily have to believe in spirit speaking to you directly to enjoy divination, and there are many ways of finding an approach that feels good to you. At the same time it feels exciting to me to explore what that actually means -- do we consider ourselves to be an interconnected part of everything else in the world? Would we describe the driving force behind the unfolding of life, death, and new life in our gardens and minds as spirit? If we do, what does it mean to be truly connected to that force, to reach beyond the chatter of our busy minds to find something more quiet and peaceful? To me the answers are yes and yes and I don't know, but I am excited to find out and engage with what I am finding in playful ways.

I don't personally believe in fortune telling in the conventional sense or that our destinies are written in unchangeable detail in the stars. I believe that we are co-creating our experiences and that we ultimately always have choices (of course we don't all have access to the same liberated choices, but that is probably a subject for another book). In that sense I feel that I have a responsibility to regularly make time and space in ritual to quieten my mind and see what guidance I can find to navigate the situations I find myself in with as much clarity and integrity as possible.

To me the vast and overwhelming complexity of this time in our lives makes these kinds of practices absolutely necessary, but of course I also understand that they have a stigma attached to them, that most people don't want to be the mad woman at the edge of the village talking to trees. How the legacy of the witch burnings still affects our ability to feel enchantment and trust our inner voice, intuition, spirit or whatever else you want to call it is also possibly a topic for another book. For now I just invite you to see how the idea of divination lands with you.

If you are curious, you could identify a question that is present on your mind and go on a walk with the intention of receiving some guidance through the symbolism that you encounter. Maybe you'll hear some birdsong that reminds you of your childhood or you'll find a little stone that feels wise and meaningful. Of course what you are finding will be coloured by your own view of the world and any judgements you might already have about a situation, but it might also allow you some quiet time to change your perspective and connect with a part of the story you haven't been intimate with yet. If the outcome is more insight then it doesn't seem important to me whether spirit spoke to you or you just chilled out enough to see things differently -- because maybe these two things are in a way also the same thing. Maybe there isn't a binary between divine inspiration and an open, creative mind.

Embodiment

What does embodiment mean to you?

To me embodiment is the opposite of just going through the motions. When I am embodied I am present, engaged and intentional. I have enough self-awareness to know my limits and am flexible enough to make adjustments as needed. I feel alive and soft and I trust that it is indeed safe to be in my body. In that sense I would always much rather do a small, doable ritual practice that feels good rather than a big operation that is so complex that I am checking out midway through. I also feel that a sense of embodiment engages my whole being rather than just my mind. I am inviting my body to set the pace and guide me towards what's needed on any given day, which feels so good. Embodiment is delicious.

A lot of the time embodiment is not a given, it is hard won. It requires the creation of spaces that feel safer and leaning into desire and truth and beauty of our own understanding. If we haven't listened to our bodies for a long time it might be hard to hear their voices at first, but that is to be expected. If we have lived in diet culture all our lives it might be hard to embrace the home we're in exactly the way it is at first, and that is also to be expected. If we have needed to check out to survive assault on our bodies and spirits it might be hard to stay present enough to feel embodied, that too is to be expected.

While disassociation is maybe something that stands in the way of embodiment, I don't want to shame it because at the end of the day, it is a sensible way to deal with something that would be otherwise unbearable if we were present with it. In my experience we can build our capacity to stay present slowly, taking one step at a time.

This predicament of wanting sensuality and embodiment but not knowing where to start and how to feel safe is well known to me. It reminds me of the saying *"the slower we go, the faster we'll get there."* Baby steps that are sustainable and feel exciting are much more effective than us throwing ourselves in situations that are dangerously far out of our comfort zone. While I have danced naked in my bedroom hundreds of times for example, I have yet to go to a contact improv class where people touch each other in spontaneous and unstructured ways (?!?) and I am glad I am giving myself enough patience to know that I am exactly where I need to be.

If you are unsure about embodiment, unsure about what it means to you, what it feels like or how you can build it that's okay. You can still have a beautiful ritual practice and a nice life. If you want you can ask yourself questions about embodiment and you can make listening to your body a priority. You can also practice forgiveness around your coping mechanisms and reach for other things that feel better.

You can unlearn & remember.

Writing and other creative expressions

To express oneself and create beauty is an inherent human desire. It feels certain to me that this is amplified in times of crisis and transition, because creativity is ultimately about experiencing, observing and then reflecting back what is true for us. I love the practice of morning pages, which is a concept popularized by Julia Cameron in her book *The Artist's Way*. The idea is to show up to your journal every morning and to fill three pages in freehand writing, bringing to paper whatever is on our minds. This writing is not meant for anyone but ourselves and it is not intended to be "good." It's just a brain dump that clears the way for other things to come through. What I write is often boring, ordinary and repetitive and that's exactly the point. I externalise some stuff that might otherwise swirl around my head for the rest of the day or even the week so that I have more focus for things that actually matter to me. In this sense, morning pages are one of my favorite creative rituals.

Making art is hard when I am feeling cranky and tired, so I am trying to keep it as easy as possible. I have a shelf and a box just for art materials and I am spending some time organising things when I have lots of energy so that everything is ready and waiting. Water colours are gentle, cheap and easy to work with and I also love embroidery, weaving, playing with natural inks, and of course, writing.

Whenever I can, I try to make something with my hands as part of my ritual practice. That way the clarity or comfort I've gained feels less fleeting because I have something tangible to take back into ordinary life with me.

In what ways could creative expression be part of your rituals? What do you "count" as art and can you expand that definition for your own freedom and enjoyment?

PART II
RITUAL PRACTICES

This part of the book will give you some more specific ideas and examples for building a ritual practice. I hope that you'll find something that works for you no matter what theme you're most keen to explore right now and that you'll also feel the freedom to customise all of these rituals in a way that really works.

Like I said in the beginning of this book, I have little experience in larger, formalised group rituals and so what I am focussing on here are simple, everyday rituals that I hope will be accessible and also effective and magical. There is a part of me that wonders if what I am suggesting is too small or too ordinary, but I am trying to remind myself that small is actually beautiful and that the depth of a ritual is often not determined by its scale and complexity, but by the heartfelt intention and presence that we can bring to it.

So in this spirit I am sharing ritual ideas for heartbreak and grief, for new chapters, for new identities and transitions, for body blessings, for creativity, and for resilience and enchantment. At this point in time these are the topics that feel most important and promising to me, and I hope I'll be back with more books on other subjects as my life unfolds.

I want to begin this chapter with a sweet & simple spell:

May you get what you need from this

May you find and rediscover a language and a practice that serves you well

May you know the power of your own magic

RITUALS FOR HEARTBREAK, GRIEF AND LOSS

I'm intentionally beginning with a section on heartbreak, grief and loss because in my experience those are the spaces in which we are most likely to turn to ritual.

When I widen my definition of what ritual is I can say that I used to have ritualised habits for times of pain that weren't necessarily helpful for me, like drinking, distracting myself to avoid my feelings or buying cheap things I didn't need. I have also had a habit of moving to new places to "start over" without actually confronting what wasn't working with the choices I had made right where I was. It took time, many years actually, to arrive at a ritual practice that makes more space for discomfort and pain and that acknowledges the power of sincere and gentle confrontation instead of avoidance.

Developing grief literacy isn't easy, but I think it's really so worth it. How we are confronting feelings of loss is a really personal, individual thing and it will look different for each of us.

The only thing we will probably all have in common is that going slow is beautiful and that meaning making may or may not occur in its own time, but cannot be forced.

I hope that as you explore the next pages you remember that even small steps towards integration and healing are big and radical.

Making literal space for grief

I think many of us don't have a sense of intimacy with good grief. We are very avoidant about death and tend to think that only Big Losses are worthy of time and space to mourn. I also don't know many people whohave experienced a funeral that felt unique and healing, which is really sad.

When I think about small, easy ways to get started with grief tending, making an altar is the first thing that comes to mind. At the beginning of the pandemic I created a small grief altar in my living room. It's still there and it's a simple and beautiful reminder that what is happening is not normal and that it's okay to cry. I covered a medium sized cardboard box with heavy navy blue fabric, then created a little stand for the death card from the anima mundi tarot deck and added a shell from the beach, a special stone and a tea light in a small recycled Nutella jar.

Whenever I feel like it or whenever I hear of someone dying I light the candle and just sit there for a moment in stillness. I could make up a special prayer or read some poetry or make some art for it, but the truth is that I am often simply too tired to do that kind of thing. What matters is that we begin making space for grief. Naming is the first magic -- just declaring that there is something to grieve is powerful, be that the species we are losing every day, the sense of certainty that has vanished, a loved one who passed away, or the end of a relationship, for example.

Many of us fear that if we start crying or grieving we'll never stop. And it's true, it might take a while to sit with our losses. It's not a one and done kind of thing. But I think what is actually much worse than crying for a while is living with the heavy weight of unacknowledged grief on our shoulders. Making a small physical space for grief in our homes is therefore an important first step.

If you'd like to try this you can find a quiet corner, place a candle there (I like mine in a protective container to symbolise a sense of shelter and protectedness in grief) and add some things that feel meaningful and soothing. It doesn't have to be big and you don't have to light the candle and sit there every day if that's too much, but it might be a nice opening. You can also write what you have lost or what the world has lost on a piece of paper and roll it up to sit there waiting for you until you're ready to feel the feelings.

There is no rush.

Letting the sea receive your sad stuff

Sometimes sadness is hard to name and share because we don't have much experience with that kind of vulnerability. Letting someone see you in your sadness is a big fucking deal. When something is weighing on me I like to go to the beach and pick a stone that feels solid and heavy in my hand, with a nice rounded shape.

I whisper something I am grieving into it, then throw it into the sea. It's a simple spell, but it's effective because it invites me to name what I am sad about while also reminding me that there is something bigger than myself (the sea!) that can hold it all, even when it feels like it's too much for me. It works in any kind of body of water - you could also do this near a stream, a river, or a lake.

Crying in the rain

Have you ever stood outside crying in little more than a t-shirt during a summer rain? It's one of my favorite heartbreak rituals. There is no need to make this complicated - simply choose something to wear that you're comfortable getting wet in, wait for a moment of rain that is not too cold or prepare for a return home to a hot water bottle and tea and then pick a quiet place to sit or stand and have a good cry. If you don't cry easily, think of something that is a gentle access point to your grief and let the rest come when it's time, no need to force it. Maybe you have lost a pet when you were little or maybe you can look up and learn about a species that has gone extinct. Whatever you choose to carry into the rain, let it open you up to everything else that needs a good cry too. I love letting my human tears mix with the sky tears and being immersed in water that runs down my skin back into the Earth.

Working with stillness

I am only just learning that a pause in a relationship can be something really beautiful. I generally need a lot of space and solitude, but I can also be anxiously attached and read silence as a thread of abandonment or conflict. I'd like to be in a space of appreciating pauses and trusting that there is a whole lifetime to relate to someone in different and shifting ways more often. I want to know that I can adapt to changing circumstances and desires. To know that there is no rush to always figure things out feels really good.

When I feel anxiety coming up, I try to enjoy pauses with more intention. To become more responsive rather than reactive, I do actually need time to process and be by myself. Keeping my hands busy with a weaving or something else that allows my mind to do some background updates can be a great ritual.

Because I love preparing, I now keep a weaving at hand as a relationship ritual when things become complicated. Whenever I need to enjoy a pause I get it out and add a few rows by hand without using the shuttle, which would speed the work up. I let my fingers lead the needle over and under, over and under until a pattern emerges. Embroidery works too -- really anything that keeps my body in simple, repetitive movements will help me process and arrive at a better understanding of where I am at, what I want and what I can contribute, without overstretching myself. Sometimes I make something specifically for the other person and sometimes I just weave or embroider aimlessly and see what happens.

Small rituals to hold ourselves

The pandemic has highlighted for me how hard I find uncertainty and unexpected change (well, I will probably mention this a few times throughout the book, so I don't mean to be dramatic about it, but it's real!). There are so many things that are completely out of our control and I think sometimes the best we can do with that is to make sure we're not abandoning ourselves, because that is something that is completely in our own hands.

At the moment I'm trying to give myself little rituals each morning and night so that I still have a sense of continuity and rhythm. This approach has been beautiful and valuable in periods of grief or heartbreak for me as well, and I'm always allowing myself to keep it small and simple. In the evening I prepare my breakfast, usually overnight oats with spices, nuts, and fruit. I start an overnight herbal tea infusion (often Nettle or Rose), put my supplements in my special dish and prepare my favorite bowl. In the morning I feel parented by my past self and have less to decide and faff with as I am arriving in a new day.

After waking up I brush my teeth, take the dogs out, look at the sea, listen to some birds or a podcast and then come home to warm socks on the radiator and my ready made breakfast and tea. This happens every day, without fail. It's so simple, but it really matters to me. Your morning and evening rituals might look different, but I wonder if you might find an intentional routine, one that maybe adapts to times of sadness, comforting too.

Remembering extinction

We're losing an unbelievable amount of species and biodiversity to extinction every year, which is such a sad and hard truth to be with. Eco-grief can be difficult to grasp for me sometimes - with how busy and detached from seasonal cycles and food production our lives have become, it's difficult to have a tangible sense of changing ecosystems "out there." Regularly learning about species that have gone extinct can be a beautiful way to become more intimate with eco-grief and grief tending in general. It might not remove a sense of powerlessness or solve climate change or environmental exploitation in itself, but it might help us develop a better understanding of what's happening and more resilience in working towards a more gentle way of being on the planet.

As often as I can, sometimes alone and sometimes as part of a group, I will research species that have gone extinct (or have been declared extinct) in the previous year. In 2019 for example we lost the bramble cay melomys, a little rodent that became the first mammal to go extinct due to rising sea levels.

What do you feel in your body as you're reading this?

What could help you in confronting these kinds of losses more often in a way that feels sad but also empowering towards action and a more radical rethinking of the way we live? Do you want to make remembering lost species a part of your ritual practice?

These are intentionally questions I am asking rather than ideas that I am presenting, because I honestly don't know. I have little glimmers of ideas and hope sometimes, but overall I feel pretty weighed down by the enormity of these losses.

RITUALS FOR NEW CHAPTERS, IDENTITIES AND TRANSITIONS

A transition is essentially the act of leaving something behind and moving towards something new. This could be a gender, a job, a new place to live, or a new way of relating to someone for example.

Without ritual it's easier to feel that things are just happening *to* me rather than *for* me, or at least with some kind of input from me. In ritual space I can go beyond pro and con lists and engage parts of myself that I might not always be listening to in order to come to a more peaceful place of clarity and trust.

In May 2017, midway through the year between my 31st and 32nd birthday, I got married to myself in Glastonbury. I was feeling under accomplished in my romantic relationships and resentful about my codependent tendencies. I was also feeling annoyed about this shift of expectations towards me as I had turned 30. It felt like being single and childless was suddenly a problem, when in my twenties it had been more acceptable as a choice. It wasn't that judgement was coming from my inner circles, but outside of them I was sometimes feeling side eyed and that sucked.

At that point self-love had been a thing on social media for years, but in some ways I was still treading water. I was compromising my boundaries and values at times and didn't always feel good about my past choices. I was appreciating or accepting parts of myself, yes, but I still had and have a path ahead of me when it comes to full on, whole body exhale, cosmic yet practical and super consistent self-love. I want to hit that sweet spot of unconditionally loving and accepting myself while also holding myself accountable to continuous and liberated learning and development in all areas of my life. I know I'm not alone.

Creating this self-marriage ritual to mark a commitment to myself before exploring any more romantic relationships felt special and important. I was embarking on my thirties and wanted to get clear with myself on what I wanted and what I had to give to myself and others. I had only gotten "engaged" in April, but the date in May felt perfect - it was the full moon in Scorpio (my sun sign) and I was able to visit one of the local wells, which aren't always open. I booked a bed & breakfast for two nights, explored a bit, ate a nice meal, and then on the evening of the full moon I took some rope, some roses, my journal and my dog

Orlando and made my way toward the Tor. It was a pretty special moon, so there were other people there watching it rise over the landscape, but that was okay.

It was already dark and I had never been there, so I had no idea how to get up the hill. I walked down the country road, found a gate that was open and followed an unlit winding path upwards. The farther we came up, the steeper it got and for the last part I had to crawl up on all fours slightly terrified of falling down. When I finally stood at the top I was covered in dirt and a bit sweaty but also totally blown away by the view and the moon that felt almost touchable.

I made a circle with my rope, sprinkled some rose petals around myself and then, while sitting at the well, read the vows I had written out loud with the moon as my witness. I couldn't imagine better accountability, because who would break a promise made to the moon? Orlando and I sat there for a bit, watched the moon being glorious and then packed up. When I noticed the path people took to go back down I laughed because it was super easy, well lit and clearly visible. I had made the way up towards this ceremony unnecessarily hard for myself, which was symbolic of so many of my relationship patterns. I didn't know better, but once I had committed to myself the path became much easier and I even saw a fox and heard some owls while walking back down.

It feels nice to think of myself as married to myself. The yearly anniversary in May is a framework to check back in on myself and an excuse to have a sweet, romantic celebration. Each year I've been asking myself where I am at in better knowing myself and building a solid foundation with my homebase from which I am relating to other people.

A few years later I also chose a new name for myself, Yarrow. I was on a holiday with my friend Myrtle and after a week of deep chill and rooftop reading in Morocco I felt like releasing my old name and starting something new. It was the January of a difficult winter, I had been sexually assaulted the month before and was in a tricky space of revisiting older trauma while also navigating the inevitable wobbles of the first few years of building a small business. This holiday was a much needed change of scenery and it really helped me shift my perspective a bit.

Changing my name was also about breaking a pattern and assuming a new identity, the identity of someone I hoped had managed to better integrate painful experiences. I had done a lot of work on myself and while there was and still is so much to learn, it was in a way a big milestone in my life. My boundaries had been crossed and I immediately drew a line, named my experience and asked for support in moving forward, which was new.

I chose Yarrow because I wildly love this plant and because its name consists of some the softest sounds in the English language. My whole body was excited about being addressed as Yarrow and I celebrated this change on a blue Moon in February that year, in the bath with a friend, swimming in Yarrow and Roses.

You might not want to get married to yourself or choose a new name, but I hope you'll find some inspiration to celebrate yourself and your transitions in this chapter.

Marrying yourself

You can make your self-marriage anything you'd like it to be, after all that is the point of having a good relationship with yourself. It can be big and shared with loved ones or small and intimate, maybe even secret. Without being too prescriptive, here are a few elements and considerations I would recommend:

Pick a date that feels meaningful to you, perhaps a special moon, your favorite season or the midway point between your birthdays. Make it a date that will be fun to celebrate as an anniversary in the future.

Share your ceremony only if you feel comfortable and try not to worry too much about what people will think.

Bring in all the things that make you feel good about yourself: favorite flowers and scents, much loved colours and decorations, your favorite outfit, and music that makes you happy.

Write vows that feel meaningful, but don't overcommit. It's okay to be exactly where you are and it wouldn't work to make promises you can't keep. Maybe you don't always totally and completely love yourself, but maybe you can commit to abundant self-acceptance and deep appreciation of all your qualities. Maybe you're not able to make time for a full on date with yourself every single week, but maybe you can make sure you have small and regular romantic rituals for yourself. At the very least commit to never again molding yourself into someone else's expectations of you at the cost of your own wellbeing.

Being able to say that I choose myself, that I celebrate myself, and that I make regular time to appreciate romantic solitude really makes a difference to how I relate to myself and others. It's reflected in the way I make my home and spend my time and in the way I deal with self-doubt and anxiety. It's not a perfect or smooth process, but it's a valid attempt to push back against diet culture, productivity worship, and sexism.

Choosing a new name

Naming is the first magic! Sometimes it's time to shed an old identity and begin a new chapter with a new name. If you feel shy about sharing yours it's okay to take a new name just for yourself, in the privacy of your home and your body and your journals. I can't really give you advice on how to choose one, but I hope the right one will come to you in a moment of soft stillness.

If you want to celebrate this new way of being in the world and claiming yourself with a ritual, I would invite you to pick elements that symbolize this new name, such as flowers, rocks, colours, scents, and maybe music that feel like a good match. Light candles and surround yourself with beauty, write about what your new name means to you, declare what parts of your old identity you are releasing, and let yourself be carried by the magic of language and words.

Home blessings & home goodbyes

At this point I must have inhabited more than 25 different houses--all kinds of house shares, sublets, dodgy rentals, and also some pretty good homes. What I learned is that moving to a new place is hard, even if it was your choice--and even more so if it wasn't.

Many people have housewarming parties and I love them, but I think home blessings and goodbye rituals can be just as important. A move so often marks the beginning of a new chapter and it feels good to remember the beautiful and difficult memories I made in a place before I move on to the next one. In my last home in Brighton I spent so much time cuddling my dog Orlando, I made out and read books, cooked meals, hosted friends and had arguments, studied new things, built my businesses, and had some very good cries. I also had some sad experiences, but they are for another book. I can't know how my life would have been different if I hadn't had those two years in the tiny house up on a hill near this small strip of woodland and all the hawthorn trees. I mean I do know that the housing market in Brighton is an absolute shit show and landlords in general should be banned so we can find new, fairer and more sustainable ways to share our living spaces, but that is probably also for another book.

My point is that I can honour what a space has offered me independent from how I came to live in it. Moving out of that tiny house after two years, the longest I had ever lived in one place, was huge. It took me three days to pack up and when I finally closed the door behind me and dropped the keys through the letterbox I felt liberated and also a bit sad. Two friends picked me up and we embarked on the long overland journey to Germany together in what I like to think of as the dreambabe express.

I said goodbye to this house by writing a letter to it and naming what I appreciated about living there. I also deep cleaned the corners and with that intentionally removed all the traces me and my dog had left so that the next person could have a fresh, clean start. On our last evening I lit candles and read through all the journals I filled while living there, then went to kiss the hawthorn trees goodbye. The moon was big and full that night, as it had been for so many of my tiny rituals on the hill.

If you find yourself moving to a new place or wanting to reclaim and remake the home you're in, make some time to think about and honour what you are leaving behind. Decluttering during a move makes a huge amount of sense, but we can also do some emotional decluttering and be intentional with what baggage we are leaving behind. Maybe there are small things you can do to give yourself a fresh start in the new place, things like donating and recycling things you don't need anymore, deep cleaning your old and new homes, spraying rose water in the corners, and opening all windows at once to let the wind blow old stuff away.

When I arrive in a new space I like to play music while I unpack, to burn some incense that feels new and fresh, and to greet the plants and trees outside my house. There is also a German belief that I love, it says that what you dream on the first night of a new home will come true. I believe in it only if and when my dreams on that first night were great, of course.

Gender rites of passage

When I got my first period I felt ashamed and confused. I hadn't expected it and didn't know much about why it came and how it worked as part of my body. When my mum noticed stains in my pants she gave me thick pads that made me feel like I was wearing diapers. It didn't feel like joining some secret club, it was just awkward. I feel a bit jealous when I hear about people who had little rituals and celebrations to mark this special moment in their lives. I think that would have helped me perceive my period as something to be welcomed, something that doesn't need to be hidden.

I also wish that these things happening in and around our bodies wouldn't carry the heavy restrictions and expectations that come with the cisheteronormative upbringing that so many of us experience. I wish we were taught our bodies are perfect and magical and that we can be anything we want to be. I wish gender was commonly understood as a universe rather than a binary and that we'd be encouraged to be open and playful in exploring our identities from the moment we are born.

I want to live in a world in which all trans folks are safe and appreciated and loved, one in which not many people remember what the word TERF (trans exclusionary radical feminist) even used to mean. I wish we all got to have rituals to celebrate a shifted or reimagined or reaffirmed gender expression and that there were no limits on what's possible.

Until we live in that world, my wish is that we create more gender rites of passage for each other and that they are loving spaces of creativity and intimacy. This could be as small and sweet as inviting a friend for dinner, making their favourite meal, and giving them a card in their favourite colour with their (new) name beautifully illustrated. It could also be as elaborate as having a coming out/into/through party for which everyone is invited to dress in their favorite, most gender euphoria giving outfit with lots of biodegradable glitter around and queer poetry being read.

If you want to make a start thinking about a rite of passage to celebrate your identity it might be nice to write about your gender, to think about things that give you joy and feel affirming and to share that with a friend. Here are some journaling prompt ideas:

How has my gender grown over the years?

What do I like about my gender the most?

What do I wish more people could see in my gender?

Of course you don't have to share any of this for it to be special if you don't feel like it. But if you do, maybe this is another opportunity to create a shared ritual space. Maybe you can make it special with tea, candles, music and storytelling. Maybe you can create the kind of environment you've always wanted for yourself and your gender in your home.

A thing I think we should all be doing is to think about how we can make our spaces inviting and safer for trans folks, especially for trans feminine people and folks of colour who are still experiencing exclusion, erasure, and violence in many communities. One of the easiest things we can do is to check our language (in spoken words, on social media, on our websites, etc.) for wording that makes assumptions about people's identities or equates genitals with gender. We can also have more constructive conversations about this, encourage each other to do better, use our voices and bodies to protect trans people, listen (really) and share our power and resources. There is no way of knowing how someone might identify or feel just by looking at them. And when we talk about cycles we of course have to remember that not all women have wombs and that not everyone who has a womb identifies as a woman.

What a gift to have people in our communities who have stories and lived experiences to share that go beyond what we have experienced ourselves. What a beautiful invitation to make embodied kindness and the radical dismantling of oppressive structures a ritual.

May we always remember that Stonewall was a riot and that it was black trans women who paved the way for queer liberation.

Letter writing as a ritual

Sometimes the sense of things still being unspoken or unacknowledged is stopping us from fully moving on when we're ready to do so. I've been there many times with many kinds of relationships and letter writing has often helped, especially when I didn't send them.

Usually I'd say yes, speaking things out and sharing them directly with the person in question is the best thing to do, but sometimes that just isn't possible. Maybe there is a boundary in place that makes sense, maybe the person has died, maybe we need to explore what we actually really want to say privately first, or maybe there is fear of not being heard or understood regardless of what we are communicating.

If one of these things is the case, I love writing a letter instead, remembering that organising my mind and expressing myself is a gift that I can give myself at any time. When I don't end up sending them I either keep them in my journal or I burn them and scatter the ashes in the sea or another special place, feeling relieved and a bit more prepared to move forward.

This ritual of letter writing really does not have to be any more complicated than that to be effective and magical, but I do think that a good pen helps. I use a cheap ink pen in dusty pink. It's price means I don't have to feel precious about it, but it does glide over the paper easily, making my writing a softer experience. This pen has seen me writing many unsaid words and it would surely have a lot to say about my inner landscapes if it could speak.

Rituals for illnesses and disabilities

In my life, periods of illness and disability have made my world smaller in some ways-- more manageable, slower, less exciting. There is grief about that, about time that can feel lost, and about the vulnerability of having unusual needs. Sometimes there is a sense of not being able to participate in life the way others can. But there is also gratitude for friends who get it, for all the solidarity and low energy hangs and the shared weirdness and wonder.

I think rituals can be a good way to mark a shift in what we can do and what we need in life. Maybe a ritual can make a diagnosis something we can claim and make our own, rather than just something that happens to us within a fucked up medical system. Maybe that feels too sad or infuriating to think about and that's okay too, or maybe all these feelings can indeed coexist.

A ritual around disability or illness could include a letter to your body about all the things you're grateful for, a letter to your friends about what you need and what you're able to give, maybe a party in which you're letting your friends help you make adjustments to your home or cook and freeze some meals. Maybe it also includes a sharing circle in which you talk about your experiences with (chronic) illness or maybe you want to start a remote book club reading work from disabled writers together. I am also creating monthly space in my calendar to intentionally connect with others who have similar experiences to me regarding social media as a way to make my phone a more nourishing thing to hang out with.

Here are some journaling prompts that might help you create your own ritual:

What kind of shift in my health or ability do I want to affirm with a ritual?

What is my relationship to this part of myself?

What do I emotionally, physically, and/or spiritually need right now, and how are my needs changing?

Once you've done some writing things that feel supportive or symbolic, something might come to mind and you might have a better idea about whether or not you want to share your practice with someone. Some people (including myself) like the idea of symbolically releasing something from their old life that they are no longer able to carry, for example the idea that we should say yes to most social invitations that we receive. I say cancel everything and throw confetti on my head sometimes! There might also be some magic in drawing new boundaries. If, for example, you know that you only want to attend future events if they have certain features, you can write that down and really affirm that you deserve that kind of access *and* that it's okay to communicate that. It might also be nice to do a decluttering ritual in other areas of your life. Maybe there are clothes that no longer fit or maybe there are aspects of your home that no longer serve you. May we find the courage to rearrange things to be more at rest.

Being comfortable is such a key value for me, really with everything I do. I'm always trying to ask myself how I and the people I love can be more comfortable, if there could be more pillows, more indirect light and candles, more accessible snacks. Fuck the idea that you have to leave your comfort zone in order to experience exciting things.

If the idea of celebrating your delight and safety feels exciting to you, maybe a nice Friday night ritual is clearing some cozy space, gathering some candles, books, chocolate and tea, turning some fairy lights on, and taking a few deep breaths. You can put your hand on your heart and affirm to yourself in sweet whispers:

I deserve to be comfortable.

It can be that simple and feel so good.

RITUALS FOR BODY BLESSINGS

Where does your body end and the landscape begin?

I'm interested in how we as humans have come to see ourselves as separate from and in charge of "nature." At the beginning of my explorations, cyclical living and a felt sense of interconnectedness seemed pretty out there to me, maybe because I had spent most of my life stressing out in big cities, not looking at the sky very much.

I was an "early developer," getting my period at eleven and observing my body change in horror even sooner than that. It was weird and unwelcome and while I didn't know exactly what those changes meant and how they would change the way men would see me, I was sure that they were not a good thing. Being a teenager was weird and exhausting and also liberating and beautiful and messy. If I had seen my body as my home then I might not have "blessed" it with quite as many vodka shots and sleepless nights, but I guess that was all part of becoming an adult human and clarity is much more sharp in hindsight. At 15 my Friday night ritual was layering my face with makeup, reshaping my breasts with wires and straps, irritating my lungs with hairspray, and downing a few glasses of cheap strawberry prosecco on an empty stomach. I was proud to walk out into the winter night freezing in short skirts and navigating the world precariously destabilized in high heels.

On good evenings I felt smug. I thought I had tricked everyone into thinking I was of legal age, that I indeed knew what I was doing. When I received an invitation flyer in the post with a picture of myself dancing on a podium with two friends I thought I had made it. It didn't occur to me that I hadn't been asked for consent and that I couldn't even remember that that picture was taken. Looking back now, I feel disgusted about the fact that the club owners made a point of decorating their parties for socialites and football players with underage girls. Finding other ways of being seen and inhabiting my body was a long process, drawn out by a lack of honest sex education and various assaults.

Towards the end of my twenties working with the moon became more of a thing on instagram and I started tracking my cycle as well as the phases of the moon. These were small, tiny baby steps for many years--reading Chani Nicholas' horoscopes, looking for the moon outside my window before bed, learning about hormonal health. I am exploring the cosmology of my body now and it means navigating a lot of unknowns.

At the same time I started to become more present to the damage that years of dieting as a teenager had done to my self-esteem and the way I share my body-home. I also began thinking about my not so great experiences with sexuality and the fact that I was so late to come out as queer. Having lived under capitalism all my life, my urge was to fix this very quickly and to see how these practices could maybe not just make me feel better about myself, but also make me a "more productive member of society." Can you see the irony?

Well, I wasn't seeing it right away. It wasn't that I said these things out loud, but retrospectively I can see that I was still applying this lens of quick fixes and productivity to everything I was trying to do for myself and my communities.

Baby steps, baby steps.

Unlearning and remembering.

I am still learning new ways of being in my body and being in the world every day, even now, in my thirties. The pandemic has forced me to be in solitude even more intensely than my introvert heart had always wanted me to be. In this loud silence of being just with myself while also riding the waves of despair and grief for the world, every little act of sincere care for my body is hard won. In the first four weeks of lockdown I needed to numb out a great deal. I ate a bar of chocolate, pizza, and chips almost every day. And I want to be clear - there is nothing wrong with that. I was coping and that's what matters. But of course it didn't really energise me, it actually made me feel even more tired.

What I am sharing in this chapter are therefore not big, elaborate ceremonies. They are small, meaningful everyday practices and rituals that you can do as special treats with relatively little time or energy. These are the things I am managing to do sometimes right now, in the midst of so much chaos.

I hope that what you take away from them is that your body is beautiful. It matters that you feel at home in it, no matter what it looks like, what your gender is, or what you can do. I know this is easier said than done, that sometimes this idea is very hard to hold. It's also really important to me to say that none of these practices are inherently gendered, though of course you can weave gender expression and celebration into them if you like. And of course anyone can relate to the moon, whether they menstruate or not.

Please give yourself time, let this reclamation be the practice of a lifetime.

May we unlearn & remember.

A mirror ritual

How comfortable are you with looking at yourself fully naked?

If you haven't done this in a long while or it makes you feel nervous you can start small by just sitting down in front of the mirror and taking a few pieces of clothing off. Maybe your top will come off, maybe just your socks so you can look at your feet.

Maybe being fully nakes feels okay today, maybe not. Arrive at a place of being seen that feels right at this time.

Then if you like you can close your eyes or rest them gently on a neutral spot. Try to soften here: see if you can release your shoulders and breathe a little more deeply. Think of an animal you truly love and care about. Maybe a bird that lives in your street or your cat or your friend's dog. Think of all the beauty and imperfection this animal inhabits so naturally and how it allows it to move through the world.

When you're ready, look at yourself with as much compassion and gentleness as possible. Think about all the things that had to come together for you to be in this place at this time in human history. Think about your beating heart, your lungs, your liver. Your ears and your feet and all these other elements of your body that play different roles in letting you be in the world in the best way they can.

Is there anything that feels hard to love or hard to look at?

If the answer is yes, you are not alone. I am still struggling with seeing traces of unwanted touch or softness that takes up space under my skin. I find that hard sometimes. It shifts and changes and it gets easier but it takes time.

Put your hand in that place that feels hard today and send your breath down through your arms into your hand, imagining gentleness arriving in that space together with your breath.

When you feel complete, slowly get dressed and move away from your mirror, but blow yourself a kiss first.

Becoming a flowery body of water

I adore thinking about the fact that our bodies are mostly made of water that circulates through us, through rivers, through rain, through plants.

I also love the simplicity and joy of making herbal teas as a way of merging with flowers and flooding my body and mind with them.

If you find yourself in need of plant support, pick one herb that is safe to consume in large quantities and drink some tea from it every day for at least 21 days. Think about your chosen flower, dream of it, let your whole body become immersed in its magic.

You can also make special tea blends to support a dream you have and pick three plants that you feel will best support your journey. On the upcoming summer solstice, I'll make a blend of dandelion (for resilience), rosemary (for clarity & truth) and calendula (for warmth & strength) and make a label that says "Abolition Magic: may we begin by tearing down the prisons inside ourselves."

Rituals of safe touch

Touch has always meant the world to me. Skin on skin contact sending showers of soft feel good hormones through my system are literally something I live for. As a baby I often had my tummy and arms stroked gently with fingernails and this sensation is still one of the things I treasure most in life, alongside the feeling of fingers running through my hair like a human comb.

Right now, during lockdown, I really struggle with a lack of hugs. I know it seems like a small problem compared to all the other problems we are facing, but I really feel it and it matters to me. I am obsessed with thinking about when we'll be able to hug again and who I'll get to hug first.

I've been leaning more into my self-massage practice and it really does help. In my twenties I trained as a massage therapist and more recently I taught self-massage as part of the Embodied Magic program because it just felt so needed. I know that for many of us, touch from others can sometimes feel unwanted, unsafe, or unpredictable for all kinds of reasons. I think that starting small, with ourselves by ourselves, can be a really good kind of magic.

What if you always had yourself to turn to for comfort and an experience of being held and touched?

In my self-massage rituals I usually begin by just sitting down at my altar. Sometimes I light a candle or put some music on, sometimes I just want stillness. And then I try to really listen to what is needed and invited. Rather than having a set routine like starting at my feet and working my way up, I am trying to see what I am being told by my body. Often I'll feel some coldness in my lower back or tension in my shoulder blades and so I start there. Gentle strokes, some pressure, being playful with circles and patterns. I rub oil I infused myself or made by friends into my skin and enjoy the warmth my hands are creating.

A few minutes can be enough, it doesn't always have to be some big operation. But I am trying to tell my nervous system as often as possible that there is safe touch and that I am open to listening and collaborating.

A spell for protection & visibility

Western beauty standards are hurting all of us, but folks of colour as well as fat, older, disabled and trans people are especially affected. I don't think many of us truly understand this spell we're living under and how much it is affecting our self-worth and what we can make happen in our lives.

Social media is a strange magic in that it's pretty new in the human world, but it already feels totally essential to who we are and how we communicate. I spent six months away from any social media last year and it felt so good. I felt like I was coming closer to myself and could hear my own voice more clearly. Less comparison, less need to perform.

A practice I would like to offer as a spell is to curate your feed into something that feels truly nourishing. As a way to separate from ordinary brainwashing you can ask yourself the following questions:

What kinds of images give me joy when I see them?

What kinds of ideas do I really want to connect with?

Whose voices am I not prioritizing?

What do I want to share and what do I want to keep to myself?

If you like you can write about these questions in your journal before you enter the liminal space of this spell, the phase in which you play with imagery.

Take some time to look through the list of accounts you follow or friends you have. If there is misalignment with the things you've identified through the questions, give yourself permission to unfollow or unfriend. There might be personal reasons for why you might not want to do that, in which case you can see if you can mute them instead so that they won't appear in your feed anymore.

Next you can research some new folks who might bring exciting new energy and ideas into *your space* (please note the emphasis on Your Space). When I returned to social media I removed a lot of folks from my feed who made me feel not so great about myself, my creativity or my body. In that I want to be clear that in most cases it actually had little to do with them and so much more with myself and the things I have internalised, which is okay.

Baby steps.

Unlearning and remembering.

I brought in some new accounts who shared about textile art and justice. I began seeing more amazing textures and colours and my brain exploded with ideas for things I wanted to try and think about. I also followed more accounts with different kinds of body types and a wider range of voices from people with identities other than my own. I had gone through a few rounds of this before, but I think that it's good to move things around and to keep returning to this ritual once or twice a year. Our interests change, the way we see ourselves changes. It's okay to let go sometimes.

It feels good to be playful in that space, to follow instinct and interest. Your feed is your own and if you know you spend a lot of time on your phone it's important to make sure you are engaging with things that feel empowering. We must remember that our bodies are always listening to everything our mind says, as well as the visuals that affirm our beliefs.

For the integration part of this ritual you can bring some awareness to how your social media experience changes over the coming weeks and how that might impact your self-image or your thoughts about what's possible and what isn't.

A ritual to get unstuck

Sometimes I wake up with a kind of heaviness in my body that feels incredibly ancient. I will leave my bed because I need to take care of my dogs, but I am incredibly reluctant and feel out of place in the world, even the world of my kitchen.

I don't always know what makes these mornings difficult, but sometimes it might be a dream I've had that I can't remember. After all the morning necessities are taken care of I snuggle back down with Orlando and Ernie and I put some music on. For this spell I made a three song playlist of music that feels uplifting, but also gentle. I danced to these three songs many times when I had more time and energy and so now, when I just lie down, listen and let myself be, I can sense a muscle memory of what it feels like to shake things out and to literally, physically, and emotionally move through something.

Sometimes I lie there and just look outside the window and sometimes I start stretching a bit, feeling my toes, running my fingers through my hair to get some energy moving.

This is a simple spell, but as you know I think those are always the best.

Water rituals

Water is the element I feel closest to and the one that makes me feel most alive and at home. I became a wild swimmer in Scotland and receive so much from being able to swim in wild, open waters with seals and oyster catchers around me. I started in September last year and then just never stopped when the water became colder. It still hurts at first when I get in, but only briefly, and afterwards I feel deeply peaceful and strong.

If there is a safe outside space to swim near you I highly recommend it, but if not there are many ways in which you can make your showers or baths more magical. In the simplest way, I love closing my eyes and imagining the shower raining warm golden light on me that washes away anything that's been stressful. I imagine some of the heaviness going down the drain and try to think of geranium soap as the divine cleaning blessing that it really is when I am letting it.

When I have more time and energy I love making a scrub from equal parts sea salt and melted coconut oil that I keep in my shower in a little black pot. You can add a few drops of essential oils if you like (please be sure you know about the safe use of essential oils though and source it sustainably) or sprinkle some dried flowers in your pot. A salt scrub is a beautiful sensory experience and a great way to wash some b.s. you no longer need away.

I don't currently have a bathtub, but when I did I loved the way hot water relaxes my muscles and literally makes me feel like a fish in the water. I know bubble baths are a self-care cliche, but they just work. What can you add to them to make it feel more like a celebration and a ritual?

When friends are having a hard time I love making them a salt bath. I'll blend some sea salt with cacao butter or coconut oil in a small amber jar, add some dried flowers and make a label on my typewriter that speaks to their situation and feels like a tiny spell in itself. When my friend turned 30 after some difficult late twenties years I made a spell bath for their birthday that included golden marigold flowers and said "your future is golden, let your twenties wash away and go down the drain." I love how cacao butter melts in the bath and leaves a thin film on our skin so that we get to carry on into the day or night with a little bit of that magic still under our skin. If you're interested in creating these kinds of bath rituals, a double boiler is something very smart to invest in. There are many videos online that will visually show you how to best combine ingredients for a bath melt or salt scrub, probably more effectively than I could in writing.

Becoming present

Pleasure and connection require a sense of presence and safety that isn't always available, especially for people who live with the impact of trauma. I want to respect dissociation as a natural response, a way in which our bodies ensure that we don't have to be present to an unbearable amount of pain or a loss of control. It can also have downsides, of course. We might check out of situations we'd actually really like to enjoy or we may become disconnected from ourselves and miss out on the beauty and joy of being truly alive to what is happening in our lives.

To me working to un-shame dissociation, to maybe even befriend it as a response that aims to keep me safe, feels like a good first step towards coming into presence. I also like experimenting with touch and movement to see what I can be present with at any point in time, and how I might expand my capacity to be here, now. This could look like sitting down at my altar and stroking my feet with my fingernails, creating tingles and trying to locate and deepen the exact sensation I am feeling. I am finding ways to say to my body *I am here with you, I am listening.*

It could also look like creating safe spaces to be playful with partners, talking in depth about boundaries and signs and desires and weird wishes like being stroked in irregular patterns with a pinwheel because that's what you're into (I am into it for sure). I want to dismantle the idea that only spontaneous, unspoken intimacy is hot and for all of us to create sensory worlds of our own.

If you are finding intimacy and presence with other humans hard, maybe you can learn more about being present with plants, animals and trees. Maybe you can sit next to a bird doing its bird thing and see if you can feel this little body in space, in relation to your own body. Maybe you can listen to sounds, observe movements, build trust with something outside of yourself. For so many of us, finding a language of true consent is new and strange, something that has to be imagined and reimagined in every encounter. But there is no wrong way of doing this and it's okay to be awkward and unsure.

Maybe you can earn your own trust by allowing yourself to start small and create moments of presence as tiny spells.

Meeting the pain

Becoming present can be particularly hard when we are living with chronic physical and/or emotional pain, especially when we are existing in an environment that invalidates our experiences. Internalising ableism and productivity culture can look like judgement or even hate for our own bodies and minds and the things they can or cannot do, which makes sense in a way and is also heartbreaking. I am interested in practices of meeting pain with gentleness and acceptance and I hope that rituals can help us get there, amongst other things like good healthcare and supportive friends.

If you are in pain right now, can you put your hands on that part of your body and breathe into it? Are there any stories entwined with your pain? If you invited the part of your body that is hurting to tell you something, what would it say and how can you listen to it?

Would it feel good to sit in front of the mirror and say to yourself *"This body is magical. My pain is valid. I deserve care."* ?

It's so easy to ignore pain when we are constantly being told that it isn't that bad and that we shouldn't be complaining about it. Therefore just acknowledging that something is hurting can be a radical act. It can open you up to making changes to your home, your schedule, your relationships, and your work that reflect how you are actually feeling and what you need.

If you are someone who struggles with cyclical pain, maybe using a tracking app could be a way for you to prepare for simple care rituals at a time when you have more energy to do this so that when shit hits the hormonal fan you have everything ready to meet yourself with kindness. I tend to crash after ovulation and experience intense fatigue and sadness. In order to prepare for this, I clear my calendar based on what my tracking app is telling me and I get ready for some intense tea drinking and film watching with zero human interactions (it is a privilege to work from home, I know).

RITUALS FOR CREATIVITY

I often find that we have a very narrow definition of what creativity is. At its core creativity is the act of creating something that hasn't been there before, which really could be anything from a nice meal to a painting. That something hasn't been there before doesn't mean it has to be unique, in some ways it has all been done before and that is okay. Stealing ideas obviously isn't okay, but becoming part of a tapestry or a lineage of artists and makers who inspire each other is awesome. What makes creativity special to me is the intention someone brings to it as well as the depth of their engagement with the process of observing, alchemising and expressing an experience.

I know this is a terrible cliche, but in that sense we are all artists. I don't see any harm in breaking down the fence around this word and letting it be for everyone who wants it. Of course there are people who make more room for a particular creative practice in their life and that's fantastic because they bring so much beauty to our communities. We should value their work and pay them fairly.

My own story with art making is pretty windy and weird and in a way I am glad about that. I wasn't particularly good at art classes in school, but I was endlessly fascinated with the prospect of doing something creative with my life. I'm a bit ashamed to admit this, but I really, really loved watching Sex and the City as a young teenager and secretly hoped to become a freelance writer like Carrie Bradshaw. I didn't necessarily desire fame or wealth, but I loved the idea of working from home, living by myself in a small and cozy apartment, and having space to share my reflections on life with others. I had experienced bullying and so there was also a desire to be seen and understood exactly the way I was, which I know in a way is something we all share. When graduation came closer I decided that me studying something creative would have been too outrageous and instead opted for a vocational, paid training that wouldn't get me into debt, the way a university education would have. No one in my family had been to university and I had no savings, so I guess it made sense that I chose something stable and more predictable.

I attended business college and worked in a bank, two things that if you know me now will hopefully seem absolutely unthinkable. Needless to say I hated it and really struggled with meeting the social expectations of these environments, but they were the ones with the most pay as part of the training. I envied my then boyfriend who went to art school and hoped to start studying creative writing part time at a distance university once I got a job, which I eventually did do.

In my twenties I slowly carved out more and more time for being creative while also holding down a very long string of shitty jobs. I took photography and writing classes and published poetry. Towards the end of my twenties, I got a grant for an MA in creative media, which I'll be forever grateful for. Zine making, web design, writing in general, podcasting, ritual design, and textile art are now important and constant parts of my life which is basically almost all I ever wanted. In a way I'm glad that I didn't go to art school after graduation, who knows what I would have written about. I don't want to romanticize a lack of access and I think everyone deserves space to create things, but I also think that I needed to have all these other experiences to really appreciate the pleasure, joy, and privilege of art making.

The rituals in this chapter are ideas that I hope will bring you closer to your own creativity whether you think of yourself as an artist or not and regardless of your experience, background or education.

Weaving or stitching for repair

I love the slow, contemplative aspect of needlework and see it as a great way to work with anxiety by keeping my fingers busy and engaged in a process of making and mending. Last year when I first moved to Scotland, I didn't know many people yet, so I had even more time to myself than usual and took some online weaving classes. My first project was a small, simple tapestry made on a lap loom. I completed it about two years after being sexually assaulted in my home in Brighton, which happened on the Gemini full moon in 2017. Anniversaries can be hard and come with flashbacks and anxiety, so I was keen to do something that would channel these feelings in a constructive direction. I also felt that I had come a long way in processing that experience. I had worked through bouts of anxiety and insomnia, left that house and moved to another country, talked about what had happened, and had therapy.

More recently I've sewn myself a simple pinafore dress made from soft cotton velvet in a shimmery forest green. Instead of a label that names its size it has a label that says *"my body is my own."* As someone who sometimes finds it hard to find clothes that fit me really well and who has very distinct sensory preferences I love having something that I really adore and made thoughtfully myself. Sewing is easier than I had imagined and while I do have a machine and learned lots about using it properly from watching videos, I want to attempt to hand stitch a garment for my next project.

Textiles are such intimate things. They are the layer of life that comes closest to our bodies almost all the time. They are the difference between an empty room and a home. Louise Bourgeois said that "the act of sewing is a process of emotional repair," which I love. I think there is a lot to think about here-- about how clothing ourselves and other according to our own actual preferences, with comfort and great fit, is an act of love. Also about how often we throw garment workers under the bus in the quest for being fashionable.

Another needlework ritual I love is making affirming embroidery hoops for my friends. I begin with a simple phrase, then choose colours and symbols that seem supportive to the message I am trying to express. They aren't masterpieces, but I enjoy the time I spent making them and I hope they express my love in a new way. I also like making patches with affirmations like *"my body is my own, my body is my home"* that you can wear inside your jacket, as a reminder and a spell for protection.

Writing with tarot cards

When I feel stuck in my writing I sometimes begin by pulling some cards and having an imaginary conversation with the archetypes I meet. It helps me in getting out of my own head and into my writing instead. Usually I begin with a good long shuffle and then draw three cards to be spread out in front of me. I'm making sure to observe any initial gut reactions in my body as I turn the cards; that's often where a lot of magic and insight can already be discovered. Sometimes a story tells itself between the three cards and sometimes I look at it more methodically as a past, present, and future spread. I really think that this is even more fun when you don't have an understanding of each card that is learned from a book, because then you can look for patterns, symbols, numbers, body language and colours in the cards and come to your own conclusions.

Whatever you're trying to write, even if it's just meant as a starting point for your morning pages brain dump, it might be nice to think of the message a card would communicate if it could speak. What would the Fool tell you about beginning a day, a new project or a new relationship? If you came to the five of cups for advice on grieving, what would you hear?

"I remember when…" or "I can see that…" are really easy, approachable page starters for so many kinds of creative writing and they can lead you beautifully into a ritual space in which you can express yourself and declutter your mind.

Zine making

I love thinking of zines as spells that can travel throughout the world to tell stories and share skills and knowledge. Zines have been made since the invention of the printing press, but have become a more popular way of self-publishing as part of punk culture. Generally speaking they are booklets that circulate in relatively small print runs and they can include anything from creative writing to photography, letters, artwork, comics, recipes, memoir, how to guides, and maps. In a way, books are very long zines or zines are very short books, depending on how you look at it. In any case you can hide inside them when things get tough and you can experience another person's world intimately or escape into some place brighter than your own. Zines gives us a chance to shift the narratives we're exposing ourselves to and to water the kinds of creative eco systems that are more aligned with our values than mainstream media.

Making a zine feels much more approachable and doable than writing a book (though I am having fun doing that too). Because there is less investment and less of the usual publishing industry gate keeping going on, it's easier to take risks and express something that needs to be said, even if it might not be commercially successful. Zines can tell stories that are often dismissed or silenced and are therefore a radical tool for healing and resistance. I love the kinds of people who go to zine fairs fairs, I love trading zines, and I love reading about things people care about.

If you want to make a zine as a ritual, a great place to start might be setting an intention. Is there a story that you really want to tell, maybe so that someone else feels less alone in their experience? Maybe you want to share a skill that is valuable to you? Do you just want to make a zine that's a little collection of artwork, kind of like a traveling exhibition that people can look at in their beds?

You can make zines with a few sheets of papers and pens and there are many Youtube tutorials about different kinds of folding techniques and decoration approaches. If you like you can also make them digitally with a free design tool and then print them. There is no need to share your zine if you don't want to - you can also make one just for yourself, maybe to officially close a chapter of your life and document something that felt big and important.

Making a zine is saying to yourself "what I have experienced or want to express matters and deserves space" and that's so beautiful.

Morning pages

I've already mentioned that I adore writing in the morning, but I feel that morning pages can be so special, they deserve their own section. In her book *The Artist's Way,* Julia Cameron recommends making time to write three pages of handwritten notes each morning and to not share them with anyone. Morning pages are not meant to be good or presentable or even coherent, they are just a brain dump that clears the way for more magical things to come through.

It really is my experience that I feel more connected to myself and clearer about my ideas, worries, desires and work when I do them every day. There is something very empowering about having this non-negotiable time to myself, irregardless of whatever else is happening around me. I find that anything else I work on later in the day flows more easily if I have cleared away some stuff from my mind by doing morning pages. If you want to try this I recommend keeping it really simple. Get a pen that smoothly glides over the page so you can write fast and get a cheap notebook so that you aren't feeling too precious about it. Then get started! Block the time in your calendar if that feels helpful or put the journal out next to your bed each night so that everything is ready in the morning. I wouldn't read back on what you wrote for at least three months as it might just end up making you feel self-conscious and hesitant to keep going.

I've written journals since I was able to write and now have a ton of material to read back through. It feels odd sometimes, but it's also nice to be able to see that things do indeed change and that I am not actually dealing with the same shit over and over again. I mean, in some ways I do of course revisit the same stuff repeatedly, but at least I can tell that there is some kind of spiral development happening that keeps me going. I think documenting life is important as it helps us develop a sense of time passing and seeds growing. Making time to write helps me to learn to trust my own mind, even if it does not operate in the way it is conventionally expected to operate. I am showing up to an empty page to develop more intimacy with my thoughts.

When I read through my business planning notebook from 2015 I see tons of anxious lists and careful calculations about small amounts of money going in and out and I can tangibly feel the anxiety I was holding my pen with. I am so glad to see now that I am no longer in that place. I make more confident decisions and I have gained some valuable experiences. Things are getting easier and I have something to prove it!

Morning pages are also a great way to explore and document your ritual practices. If you are experimenting with the elements of ritual I shared in part one of the book to create your own rituals it might be nice to build up your own little guidebook to refer back to by integrating that into your morning pages. I have so often created rituals and thought I would remember them, but they often slipped away and I didn't make enough time and space to reflect on them.

Digital collaging

I know there is something very special about working with your hands, cutting stuff up and pasting segments back together, but for times when this isn't possible I think having a little digital space for future dream rituals can also be beautiful. I like creating boards on Pinterest because the app allows me to work with them while in bed or traveling, making it a more low energy and more portable activity. Pinterest is my platform of choice because it's easy to manage different boards with different themes and also because it feels less interactive and therefore distracting and overwhelming compared to spaces like instagram.

Before I moved to Scotland I made a vision board for my life here and called it *"living the middle aged dream in Scotland."* I was tired of expensive urban living and wanted something small and slow, close to beautiful landscapes and full of sheep, yarns, and washed out colours. Looking at this board got me through the long summer of trying to find a rental here and it now makes me feel proud to look back at it and see that yes, some of these things did actually come true. And I am ready for more of them.

It doesn't have to be a new country, but maybe there is an area of your life that you do want to "develop" in some way, without any outside pressure for relentless self-development. If the answer is yes I hope visualising your ideas will be a helpful ritual in getting you there.

RITUALS FOR ENCHANTMENT AND RESILIENCE

Resilience and enchantment feel like two closely related kinds of magic to me because I can draw so much strength from still feeling enchantment in times of difficulty. As I write this I'm nearing three months of living alone in lockdown with minimal contact to other people, at least offline. It's been hard at times to enjoy this as some sweet solitude rather than loneliness and it has of course brought back up older, unrelated feelings of abandonment.

I know that I am lucky, lucky to have a safe home now, to have access to nature and two loving dogs to hang out with, amongst many other things. Being in nature and being really present with my dogs rather than just looking after them has time and time again pulled me out of the slump that came with being inside my own head so much more than usual. There is a sense of intimacy with this landscape here and more of a feeling of belonging that I haven't known before, and that really makes all the difference. In the absence of dinners with friends or hugs there are still beautiful things to explore and to be inspired by.

When I was sexually assaulted two years ago, I froze. I had a really hard time sleeping and consequently became hypervigilant, restless, and anxious. Thawing took time. It took a lot of walking amongst hawthorn trees, seeing seasons change, lying under my weighted blanket, and baking cinnamon cookies. It was a process of reassuring myself and my nervous system over and over again that it's safe to be present, to come home.

I think this being present is crucial for our movements as well. I don't want to just be reactive anymore. I don't want to only make "donations" when something bad happens, when another black person is killed by the police. It's not good enough. I want to have the capacity to stay present and fully engage for the rest of my life, to be able to hold complexity and discomfort and to know that sharing power is possible, necessary and safe. I want to and need to be able to respond from a rooted place so that I'm able to be wrong, to better listen and learn and to act in integrity. I also want to find faith in something that is inside of myself, inside of my communities and the landscapes I am part of.

Of course enchantment looks different for everyone. My hope is that some of these notes might help you become clearer on what it means to you and how it can become more present and touchable in your life. In some ways we know so little about what is coming next, which is hard, but I do think that all possible futures will benefit from enchantment and resilience.

Small commitment ceremonies

I am still learning about how to maintain a sense of enchantment in long-term romantic relationships as well as in friendships and family relations. Right now I am thinking about how much I miss hugs several times a day. I cannot, absolutely cannot wait to wrap my arms around another human being and breathe together and giggle and then cry about how we've missed this. Hugs, when they are mutually wanted, can feel like such a beautiful affirmation of closeness and connection.

Anyway, what I actually mean to write about in this section is how much I love small commitment ceremonies (can you tell I really miss hugs though?). Conventionally there is only one form of relational commitment that we formally celebrate: a wedding. Weddings can be cute, but I think it's liberating to widely broaden our excitement about celebrating all kinds of big and small commitments.

I'm excited about relationship anarchy, the idea that we can create and re-imagine all kinds of relationships with all kinds of people outside of heteronormative boxes and compulsory monogamy. With that we might still have to work with the often limited amounts of time and energy we have and we might also still choose monogamous commitments if it's right, but we can love more freely and don't have to get all our needs met from just a very small circle of humans.

I love friendship. I love the excitement of meeting someone new and deciding to be friends because omg we have so much in common and there is so much we could do together. I also love the familiarity and comfort of knowing some of my friends for a really, really long time. Having seen each other through decades of our lives, knowing so many of each other's secrets, cooking favorite meals for each other on sad days. What a gift.

In the last few years I've created commitment ceremonies with some of my friends that were really beautiful declarations of love and investment in each other's wellbeing. I don't think that our commitments have to be huge for them to be worth celebration or that we have to make lifelong promises. I promised to one of my friends that I'll always share my special snacks with them and that was so incredibly meaningful because we both love luxury snacks and have experienced financial hardship in our lives that at times made them impossible.

A commitment ceremony can be as simple as picking a special date, dressing up, lighting some candles, and saying out loud what we love about each other. We can commit to always telling the truth and to listen as best as we can. If we really mean it, we will be able to give and receive more than many people ever will.

Do you feel weird about asking your friends to do a small commitment ceremony with you? If so, can you say why it feels weird?

I know it did feel weird for me at first. But one of my top ten queer agenda items is normalsing romantic friendships and unconventional human constellations. I like throwing "I love yous" around like confetti and I like knowing that I can experience intimacy, joy, mutual aid, inspiration, and comfort in lots of different settings, even as an introvert who really is happiest at home.

Making a local plant friend

What makes you feel like you belong? The way we relate to one another, the way we choose a place to live, and the pace with which we make decisions has changed so much. To me having a sense of belonging makes the difference between being able to enjoy solitude and feeling lonely. And of course belonging can mean so many things: having a reliable circle of friends, not worrying about being deported, feeling like we are integrated in a local community, feeling seen and appreciated, being able to navigate the culture we're living in with ease, or knowing there are people and places we can always turn to for support and company.

I've moved a lot around, especially in my twenties. Wherever I went I tried to get to know a few local plants, even if I am by no means particularly good at plant identification. In every landscape there are creatures that are abundant, resilient and friendly. Where I live now there are seas of dandelion on my street and all the way down to the beach. They close their flowers in the night and open back up big and bright yellow when the sun shines. They also grow through concrete, take up space, and add splashes of colour everywhere.

If you are wanting more rituals that bring a sense of belonging, try to get to know your local plants. Pick litter, bring them treats that they love, read poetry to them. Let them know you're there, that you want to be part of their network, and that as a human you understand you have a lot to learn about belonging and reciprocity.

Inhabiting an archetype

The tarot is full of powerful, strong, and resilient characters that speak to us through symbolism. When I am wishing to embody a particular quality more often in my life I'll pick a card that I feel has that exact characteristic.

For example, after a period of unexpected change (a Tower card moment), I might choose to work with the Star card, which I associate with re-orientation and post-traumatic growth.

I'll place the card on my desk or my altar and once a week sit down to just meditate with it before I shuffle my deck and draw two cards, one about what I can do to get closer to the embodiment of this archetype and one on what I can let go to be more like the Star. I write a bit about it and document my relationship to this card over time to trace the shifts in how I experience my situation.

Forests as altars, oceans as temples

I know many of us, queers especially, carry religious trauma and might not have places of worship in which we feel truly at home, safe, and welcomed. Of course it's okay to not even want them, but if you do miss a place to come for contemplation and stillness then it might be nice to find a space of natural beauty near you and make it your own place of worship.

It doesn't have to be a dramatically stunning forest clearing or a far away river running down a magical mountain, it could just be a tree you feel particularly drawn to in your local park or in your garden or a special quiet spot near a lake or at the beach.

If you can, try to visit it throughout the seasons and note how it changes over time. It might teach you about the cycle of life and death. Notice how the colours change, what kind of animals come to nest, how they go about their days and what sounds you can hear. Think about what you can bring to this place as an offering and keep it simple and helpful, like picking litter or hanging up some bird food.

When I started wild swimming I suddenly felt so much closer to oceans and wanted to learn more about how to protect them. Of course I had known about things like micro plastic or oil spills before, but I felt so much more detached from these things. I think that sweet spot between being frozen in panic and helplessness around environmental destruction and engaging with what we can do in a responsible way is really hard to find unless we do have some sense of knowing our place in the world. When

I swim I understand I'm not actually so separate. I know I have to wait for the tide coming in for it to be safe, pick a time when the wind isn't too strong, make sure my body won't cool down too much and make sure not to step on little crabs.

Near my home beach there is a small road you can follow towards the cliffs and it brings you to what I like to call the wild place. It's not a huge area, but a small and beautiful cliff formation that is the home of many noisy birds. If you turn toward the sea it feels like you are miles away from anything human, but if you turn the other way you can see the rows of Victorian houses, children playing at the beach, and brave people swimming. At the moment the primary colours of this place are deep, rich greens and washed out shades of pink and purple. You can walk along the little path and let your fingers run over the long, soft grass. You can also watch the sea change from a mellow, still body of water to a foamy, wild arrangement of waves when the wind comes. Being there by myself is the closest thing to transcendence I know.

Rituals for mutual unshaming

Shame is a terribly crushing feeling to hold and also something that has been strategically weaponized against marginalised folks. Growing up I kind of instinctively knew that feminists were seen as angry, annoying women in many spaces outside of my family. I can't say exactly where I picked that up, but I remember clearly that I knew it was shameful to be seen as a woman with visible body hair, to desire other women, or to be angry about something, really anything. I knew we were expected to be agreeable, hair free, kin, and caring--even if no one explicitly told me this.

I also knew that it was shameful to be overweight, unable to do something other people could easily do, or to not be able to buy things peers could afford without a second thought. Adulthood didn't turn out to be shame-free either; I encountered shaming in the performance and productivity culture of all of the workplaces I sold my time at.

Maybe when we love someone, one of the best gifts we can give them is to help them un-shame. To let them know we're up for seeing their uncertainty and doubt and the way they just cannot accept some parts of themselves and still love them. What does it take to create relationships with such a solid foundation of trust that we can be completely ourselves and tell the truth without fear?

Shame leads to a particular kind of self-consciousness that stops so many beautiful people from freely creating what they're here to create. When I say "create" here I mean really anything: books, homes, paintings, communities of care or small businesses for example. It further perpetuates marginalization because it silences the kinds of voices we most desperately need right now. We need to hear stories from people who understand the magic of liminality, of resilience, of weaving healing and art together in reciprocal relationships.

What might be a ritual you can do with loved ones to share your un-shaming? I like making ritual space for mutual active listening as a healing practice. Usually I would invite a friend to talk about a specific theme that feels present and a bit shameful for both of us, for example money and debt. Then we create a space together that feels good on a day that we both have time and energy and add little treasures like special snacks, soft music and candles. Each person then gets 15 minutes to talk about their stories, ideas and feelings of shame around the topic while the other person just listens with unconditional positive regard and real openness. At the end we each decide if we want feedback or we might choose to just say something like "*I see you, thank you for sharing your experience. I am wishing you freedom from this shame.*"

It's so simple, but so powerful.

Deepening intimacy with what we already have

I think it's human to reach for something to buy when what we feel is unbearable. Well, I think at least it's human for someone who has lived under capitalism all their lives. We all know the quick rush of dopamine or the almost automatic "yes, please" to being told that we can buy something to fix ourselves or the situation we're in. That was my default mode as a teenager buying fast fashion every time my self-esteem took a hit or I just didn't know what to do with myself. And it still happens sometimes when I've had a sad day. It makes me feel better for five minutes and then it fades.

Empowering purchases are the ones I've made clear headed, in alignment with my values and ideally in support of another small business. I love it when things last a really long time and I get to be intimate with something that surrounds me. I'm not a fan of shaming working class folks for hoarding stuff or buying things that wont last long (you know, because not everyone can afford $20 beeswax wrapping paper), but I do really like the idea of being able to touch everything we own, which was popularized by Marie Kondo. I've done this as part of a moving houses ritual several times and while it certainly made moving houses a more drawn out, faffy process it also did really help me to appreciate all the things I do already have. The first time I did it was probably the biggest act of decreasing my belongings and donating clothes and books I wasn't using anymore. Subsequent moves brought smaller waves of simplification and alignment with them.

In addition to helping me understand and feel the abundance of what I have, it also helped me to be more discerning with any new things I have brought into my home because I have a better overview and can decide how things will fit together. Before I started doing this I might have bought a second watercolour set when I didn't remember that I already had one, or bought garments in a wild colour that I have nothing else to go with. Knowing what is around me also helped me understand what I value in things-- complete colour coordination everywhere, natural materials, and pleasing textures.

I'm keen to make more things myself, source them locally, or at the very least better understand how they are made and how I can pay for them fairly. If this seems exciting to you too, a great ritual might be to pull everything out of your wardrobe, sort out what you are no longer wearing to recycle or donate it, and then lovingly fold everything back up. Putting things together in a way that makes sense might make you feel that you do actually have things to wear and are clear on what you enjoy on your skin.

A ritual of tending to our belongings can of course be great for any kind of item, books, art materials and trinkets deserve love and attention too.

Dark Moon Magic

The dark moon graces us with its invisible presence just before the tiny sliver of a new moon appears in the night sky. Its magic is that of turning inward and being intimate and cozy with the absence of light, of seeing and knowing. It's hard to not know. We value cerebral highs and fast data and so we're often freaked out by things that remain a mystery, like death.

But rebirths, reimagination, and reclamations necessitate death to come first, to clear space and prepare the soil for something new to grow.

I was born under a balsamic moon, the very end of a moon cycle, under a Scorpio sun--all elements of the sky that are about death, cosmic darkness and turning inwards, so I'm passionate about getting more people excited about their value and magic.

The dark moon is a time of dreaming and resting to me and I'm always trying to go extra slow, to make even more time for dark chocolate and luxurious beach walks. This is the space in which I have the best ideas. Sometimes when I feel stuck around a situation I try to wait until after this cozy dark moon time, my home base, to revisit it again. When I do I always see things in a different light.

My favorite ritual practice for the dark moon is to create a literally dark cave for myself. I draw the curtains, block all light as best as I can and just light some candles. Sometimes I play soft music quietly, but most likely I'll just be in silence. I hang out in my favorite soft black underwear and rub oil all over my body before I meditate and allow myself some stillness. Then I'll draw a few cards, write my reflections about them down, and prepare some mugwort tea that I'll drink before bed. Mugwort is thought of as a dream plant that can help us have illuminating dreams. If I have something on my heart that feels a bit uncertain or worrying I might write a question on a piece of paper and place it under my pillow together with a little bit of dried Mugwort. In the morning I'll have my journal ready and write down what I dreamed of and think about how it might relate to my questions.

I like this process as an exercise in handing over control and not trying to "fix" everything with my conscious mind, but to get creative and allow for non-linear exploration in the darkness of the moon.

Finding a good place for your inner child

When big feelings come up in ritual practices (or anywhere really), it sometimes feels like ancient wounds are opening back up again and it stings. It might sting because there is a part of us that remembers neglect or bullying or because we feel shame for having needs that aren't being met. That can be a very real, and present experience of course, but it can also be something that belongs to our childhood.

Maybe inner child work seems abstract or new agey for you, that's okay. I think of it just as a way to openly and honestly interact with the parts of our younger self that are still with us today and have their own wisdom and insights to share. It's strange to me that we create this hierarchy between people at different stages in their lives--how youth is so celebrated and yet children are denied much agency or how we do really crave wisdom and experience, but shame women for getting older. I think there is no stage of life that is inherently better or worse than any other and that each phase has its own magic and its own challenges. I certainly wouldn't want to be a teenager again for example, but I can respect that I had a talent for freely expressing my moods and questioning authority with abandon.

If you're interested in thinking about how you can integrate and honour all parts of yourself, maybe it would be nice to create a small inner child ritual that you can turn to whenever you feel a past sense of insecurity or worry coming back up. One way of doing this is to find a quiet place to lie down and to have pen and paper ready in case you feel like writing after doing this little meditation. Bonus points if you also have your favorite childhood snack or can listen to a song you used to love. Take a few minutes to just breathe deeply and connect with your body, coming to a space of knowing that there is nothing to fix. You are okay exactly as you are and it's okay to have needs. Next, think about a good childhood place--a space in which you have made only happy memories and that you enjoy returning to in your mind. This could be a beach you went to on a holiday, a tree house, a corner of the playground you loved, the desk you did your first drawings on or really anything else that feels good. Really visualize this place in detail - try to remember colours, textures, sounds and whatever else comes to mind. If you can, bring this memory more into the forefront of your mind, as if you are pulling something out of an archive to be used again.

Once you have explored your memories to a level of depth that feels good to you you can put your hand on your heart and imagine "locking in" that memory so that you can return to it by guiding yourself into this simple meditation any time you feel like it.

PART III
CREATING A REGULAR PRACTICE TO LEAN INTO

I wrote this book because I needed something to lean into myself and because I wanted to share my enthusiasm for rituals and a politicized practice that emerges from our own understanding and inner power. I'd like to be part of a conversation about spirituality that embraces queers, one that centers justice, and one that meets us where we are--cynicism, doubt and fear included.

As I've mentioned many times, I am a big fan of simplicity and would always choose small daily rituals created with devotion over occasional larger ceremonies. 2020 asks of me to look for what is available and possible and nurturing more than any other year. I found that seeking beauty in ordinary things has an important place in making sure we're meeting this moment with as much grace and integrity as possible.

Last year I set out to learn more about cyclical living and death awareness and now here we are, confronting these things head on. I hope that what I have shared has given you some fluid inspiration that you feel confident you can shape into something that makes sense for you.

Now that you've read about some of my ritual practices, what are you most excited about trying for yourself?

What would make you feel more creative, grounded, and supported in your life?

What does it mean to start small where you are and grow from there?

I'd like to say a few more things about habits and change that I hope might be useful. I am someone who has taken an incredibly long time, many many years in fact, to really make ritual practice a central part of my life. I have always known, since I was little, that I love ritualised creativity and play and that I need these things to be okay on the most basic level. And yet I have spent many years chasing other goals and resisting confronting my feelings as hard as I could.

It just takes time. It takes time to change things and many of us have to fight hard for small pockets of privacy and headspace and energy to make something just for ourselves. I am in love with the idea that sometimes over time discipline becomes devotion. A friend once asked me how to tell the difference between discipline as self-care and discipline as self-harm and honestly I thought that was one of the best questions I've ever heard. It is pretty hard to answer yet so important to feel into. The more you practice the more you'll develop your discernment and be able to tell how much structure you need in your life at any point in time, at least that is my experience.

Sometimes I really want something and I know in my heart that it will be good to stick with it, but making it a habit still feels like running up a hill. This book feels so different because I am devoted to it. I get up at six every morning, I sit down to write, and I bring at least a thousand words to the page whether I have something to say or not. I've made a deal with myself and the universe and I am receiving lots of support and synchronicity during a time of crisis in return. I am so grateful for that.

There are a lot of things falling away right now. Mostly this happens by force--we are in lockdown and so many things we have taken for granted are no longer within reach. Most of us don't hug our friends, we're not travelling, or sharing meals, or goinf to the museum. We're just home, being with our thoughts and families and pets and worries.

I'm trying to stay present to the truth of what's happening, to not look away from the horror, the impact and the number of people dying, but it isn't always possible. It's just a lot more than I can handle if I am being honest with myself. This is probably the biggest both/and situation of my lifetime because there are also things that are tenderly hopeful. So many people all of a sudden get involved in mutual aid projects, build relationships with their neighbours (from a distance) and question centralised power structures.

There is talk about a legal right for folks to get to work from home, something disabled people have been campaigning for for ages. Statues of racist slave owners are finally being taken down. Local organic farmers now have waitlists for their vegetable boxes and lots of people are talking about all the things they realized they don't actually need or would be willing to share moving forward. I'm wondering if there is an element of bargaining happening, something like, "if I get to survive this, if my loved ones will still be here, then this is what I am willing to give up."

And then there is also crushing, violent injustice. Working class people are being told to get back to work, but can't send their kids to school or use public transport safely. Police violence is rampant and even more black people have died at the hands of cops. Many folks with zero hour contracts or precarious gig economy work are still waiting on government support. In debates about which corporations or industries we should be bailing out there is little talk about the real costs to marginalised communities, to regions that will be the hardest hit when we keep consuming and flying and producing waste the way we have. People are allowed to see their bosses again before they get to see their families.

We are beginning to feel the impact of climate change under our skin and we have a very small window to act and turn large future disasters into smaller ones. There is exciting research happening into the most effective ways of communicating risk because we're seeing that simply telling people that if they do x then y is going to happen doesn't necessarily motivate us to change our ways.

I'm hoping that maybe in addition to facts and information, it is helpful to also embrace more ritual practices that nurture resilience and enchantment. That maybe all of us feeling the sweet tingle of walking in the forest at night more often will make visible what we stand to lose in a more tangible way. That it also gives us the strength to keep going towards change in personal and collective spheres because fucking hell, the path to justice seems long.

I mean, which other global pandemic should we wait for before we radically distribute wealth and share power in earnest? I don't know. I am often caught between cynicism and hope and in those moments I find that harm reduction, embodied solidarity, and art making are the best things I can reach for. I want to honestly and intensely question what I am doing with my life. I want to know, with every aspect of my being, that we need change on large, structural levels, that the era of billionaires and state violence has to end. I want to also see that structures are made of people and that my own small actions matter. We are interconnected parts of this and what we do has an impact, even if capitalism has created so much separation between us and the distant cycles of production and harm we benefit from.

To bring this back to the title of this chapter: what regular practices do we need to keep going right now, to love each other well and to stay present? What do you need in your life to move through this time with as much compassion and grid as possible?

I'm not saying that it will be all ritual and rose pedals. I think it will be a lot of complexity and doubt and protest and beauty and hardship and solidarity.

Some of the books that have inspired my practice and my writing

- *Braiding Sweetgrass* by Robin Wall Kimmerer
- *Caliban and the Witch* and *Re-enchanting the World* by Silvia Federici
- *Pleasure Activism* and *Emergent Strategy* by adrienne maree brown
- *The Wild Edge of Sorrow* by Francis Weller
- *Dreaming the Dark* by Starhawk
- *Upstream* by Mary Oliver
- *The Natural Death Handbook* by Nicholas Albery and Stephanie Wienrich
- *The Power of Breath* by Jennifer Patterson
- *Writing Down the Bones* by Natalie Goldberg
- *Women Who Run With the Wolves* by Clarissa Pinkola Estes
- *The Heart of Trauma* by Bonnie Badenoch
- *She is Sitting in the Night* by Oliver Pickle and Ruth West
- *The Body is not an Apology* by Sonya Renee Taylor
- Period Power by Maisie Hill
- On Weaving by Anni Albers
- The Artist's Way by Julia Cameron
- On Being an Angel by Francesca Woodman

- Intuitive Herbalism by Nathaniel Hughes & Fiona Owen
- Boundaries & Protection by Pixie Lighthorse
- Love without emergency by Clementine Morrigan

About Yarrow

I live a soft, slow life in a village on the East coast of Scotland and create rituals for big and small milestones in life. In addition to being a celebrant I also write, make textile art, host two podcasts (Daydreaming Wolves and the DIY Business podcast), swim in the sea all year and do a lot of queer dreaming.

I'm happiest reading by candle light in a cuddle pile with my two dogs.

You can support my work by sharing it and/or becoming a patron at Patreon.com/DaydreamingWolves which gives you access to my other writing as well as live workshops, recordings and programs.

Read more and get in touch at YarrowMagdalena.com and YarrowDigital.com

Thank You

Thank you to Sophy Dale for being a wonderful writing mentor and to Coco Detrow for doing such kind editing.

Thank you also to so many beautiful beings who have directly or indirectly taught me about the value of ritual -

Orlando, Ernie, Marissa Correia, Dori Midnight, adrienne maree brown, Chanelle Bergeron, Clementine Morrigan, Lara Veleda Vesta, Pixie Lighthorse, Myrtle, Rebekah Erev, Otter Lieffe, Anja van Geert, Danette Relic, Lisa Nagel, Brunem Warshaw, Nancy Antenucci, Manisha Tare, Julia Cameron, Jennifer Patterson, Eryn Johnson, Sarah Kerr, Nisha Moodley, Lisa, Ren Zatopek, brontë velez, Adrienne Sloan, Marina, Matti, Natalie Novak, Alexis J. Cunningfolk, Miel Rose, Allison Carr, Asali Earthwork, Milla, Chani Nicholas, Natalie Goldberg, Kathleen Callahan, Clarissa Pinkola Estes, Francesca Woodman, Starhawk, Octavia E. Butler, River Jones, Finn Oakes, Robin Wall Kimmerer and many others.

Lightning Source UK Ltd.
Milton Keynes UK
UKHW021826300820
369074UK00016B/455